Dear Robert,
I admire your
social work field.
thrived in this
for helping and training others. I
am also fascinated with your
involvement for the health of
children affected with HIV/AIDS.
You're a true inspiration.
Cynthia Eyeshemitan

Robert,
Thank you for being a
pioneer for vulnerable
youths and children in
building tools & strategies
to aid others in social
work. As you read
our book, May it remind
you of our shared
Passion.
McCauley
30. Jan. 2022

Endorsements

When authors follow social issues based on their own life and work experiences, it lends an additional level of credibility to the subject matter and a perspective that few other people can present.

Given the current state of the child welfare system in Canada, and more specifically Manitoba, I think this book has identified and brought to light the importance of providing child welfare services from a holistic perspective when addressing the issue of sexual violence, addictions, and domestic violence (SAD). With the passing of Bill C-92, it is imperative that policymakers begin to take into consideration the generational effects of SAD on the lives of children and families.

As a social worker and academic with experience working in various levels of the child welfare system, I recommend this book because it begins to address a very controversial topic and social issue, which makes it true to the core value of the social work profession (social justice).

Ithan Bullard
PhD student, MSW, RSW, MHT

Well-researched and a good chronological documentation of the evolution of the Child and Family Authorities Act in Canada today and its influences, both positive and negative, from previous systems such as the Poor Law Amendment Act, Elizabethan Poor Law, British poorhouses (a.k.a. workhouses), and current Child and Family Services Laws. The thought provoking and poignant question posed by the authors throughout the manuscript, "is this truly a service or a dis-service?" is a legitimate question to ask.

I commend the authors for shining a bright spotlight, through professional, objective, and experiential lenses, on a system that has impacted so many children and adults and will continue to do so. It has to be thoroughly monitored, assessed, and carefully modified to ensure positive outcomes.

As a minister of the gospel, this passage from the Gospel of Matthew chapter 25, verse 40, comes to mind when dealing with the less fortunate and often forgotten among us: "… Verily I say unto you, inasmuch as ye have done it unto one of the least of these my brethren, ye have done it unto me."

I wish you all much success in being champions, agents, and angels of change!

Pastor Dr. Brian Archer, PhD, P.Eng.

I salute the courage of these young women. It takes courage to create change and to attempt to do things differently. Undaunted by the system, their diversity, and cultural differences, they have attempted to create a solution to a problem that has become a global anomaly.

Violence, addiction, and crime all stem from the poor quality of family systems that have been identified in so many societies. Many of the children who are at risk of violence, abuse, and addiction from their primary caregivers are placed in the child welfare system to give them a better chance at life. However, the statistics show that despite the *intervention*, the numbers are rising. More children are growing into adult youths who are homeless, without a steady income, in jail, or hooked on drugs.

From an objective perspective, the authors critically examine the current Canadian child welfare system, and with their experience in social work and based on their study and research, they have identified the problems with this system and have attempted to proffer solutions that can create change.

Based on verifiable facts and research, the authors have written a book, *Child and Family Dis-services: Objective Perspective Inside the System*, that boldly outlines the issues and links the majority of recalcitrant young adults in the society as those who have gone through the child welfare system. Some of their facts are shocking, but facts are only a reflection of the truth.

They state the reasons why the child welfare systems have not worked as effectively as they were created to and proceed to outline solutions that are advised for policymakers to review and subsequently adopt.

This book is not only relevant to the Canadian government and people, but should be studied and dissected by people all over the world, and is instructional for every society or community that wants to see their children raised in a loving, safe environment, and grow into adjusted and well-balanced young adults.

Dr. Aisha Tosan, DBA, MSc, PhD
Executive Director, Bi-Communications,
Presenter, Crime Fighters

Child and Family Dis-services:
Objective Perspective Inside The System

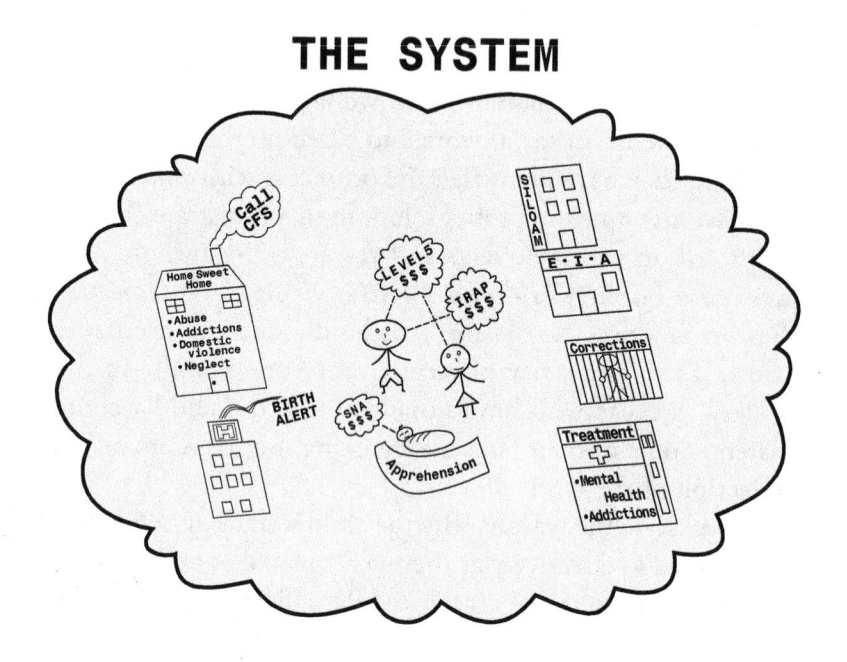

THE SYSTEM

Child and Family Dis-services: Objective Perspective Inside the System is the first in a four-part series of books regarding child welfare. The following are the upcoming titles in this series.

Child and Family Dis-services: Who Will Save the Children?

Child and Family Dis-services: It Takes a Village to Raise a Child

Child and Family Dis-services: Who Will Train the Workers?

CHILD AND FAMILY DIS-SERVICES: OBJECTIVE PERSPECTIVE INSIDE THE SYSTEM

CYNTHIA EYESHEMITAN,
COLLEEN MCCAULSKY,
&
KAREEN THOMPSON

AUTHOR ACADEMY elite

Child and Family Dis-services: Objective Perspective Inside the System

Printed in the United States of America

Published by Author Academy Elite
PO Box 43, Powell, OH 43035

Copyright © 2020 Kareen Thompson.

All rights reserved. This book contains material protected under International and Federal Copyright Laws and Treaties. Any unauthorized reprint or use of this material is prohibited. No part of this book may be reproduced or transmitted in any form or by any means, electronic or mechanical, including photocopying, recording, or by any information storage and retrieval system, without express written permission from the authors.

Identifiers:
LCCN: 2019918014
ISBN: 978-1-64746-006-8 (Paperback)
ISBN: 978-1-64746-007-5 (Hardback)
ISBN: 978-1-64746-008-2 (Ebook)

Available in paperback, hardback, e-book, and audiobook

All Scripture quotations, unless otherwise indicated, are taken from the Holy Bible, New International Version®, NIV®. Copyright © 1973, 1978, 1984 by Biblica, Inc.TM Used by permission of Zondervan. All rights reserved worldwide.

Any Internet addresses (websites, blogs, etc.) and telephone numbers printed in this book are offered as a resource. They are not intended in any way to be or imply an endorsement by Author Academy Elite, nor does Author Academy Elite vouch for the content of these sites and numbers for the life of this book.

Book design by Chris O'Byrne, Cover design by BlesseD'sign

In loving memory of:

The late Ms. Darla Spence of the Cross Lake Community in Manitoba, who was instrumental in Cynthia's professional growth in the field of child welfare.

The late Mrs. Millicent Thompson, a grandmother who played a significant role in helping to raise Kareen into the strong, kind, loving, and caring woman that she has become.

The late Herbert George McCaulsky. We pay homage and tribute to a tremendous influencer and supporter of the conceptualization, endorsement, and the near completion of this book project. As a mentor and confidante to his sister Colleen, his words echo and resonate in all of us, that whatever the mind conceives, that it can achieve. His greatest desire was to see the publication of his author sister's book but succumbed to an unfortunate and untimely death due to the COVID-19 pandemic. Mr. McCaulsky has passed but his legacy and ideologies for social injustice lives on.

"The bond that links your true family is not one of blood but of respect and joy in each other's life."

—Richard Bach

TABLE OF CONTENTS

Part ONE: Re-Formed Child Welfare　　　　1

Chapter One: Child Welfare Past and Present......... 3
Chapter Two: Entering the System 16

Part TWO: Villainy in the Village　　　　23

Chapter Three: Cash for Care................... 27
Chapter Four: Preparing to Exit the System 40

Part THREE: The system dependency cycle: will it ever change?　　　　47

Chapter Five: Transitioning into Other Systems 49
Chapter Six: The Cycle Continues. Who Is to Blame? .. 60

Recommendation............................. 65
Conclusion 71
Appendix.................................. 73
Bibliography 77

LIST OF ILLUSTRATIONS

Diagram .... Page#

Table A: changes in child welfare laws over different eras....4

Table B: past and present child welfare laws.............10

Table C: explanation of the SAD pandemic.............12

Illustration of entering the system....................16

Picture of village raising the child 24

Picture of children being priced in the system...........27

Diagram of micro, macro, and mezzo level systems.......32

Picture of different systems that youths transition into ... 48

PREFACE

We believe that to influence change is to bring awareness among the population via education on the effect of the SAD pandemic on the individual, families, communities, and society. Changes loom within the Canadian child welfare system, and people need to have an inside perspective of what is transpiring in order to make the decisions that will bring about positive changes for children and families. It would be beneficial for members of the public to receive an objective view from individuals who have spent many years on the front line providing direct services to children and their families. And since print and electronic media are unofficial policy actors in influencing public action towards social changes, this book provides valuable knowledge and insight.

Policymakers will understand the need for the child welfare system to be restructured from the micro, macro, and mezzo levels and to make unbiased decisions that will impact the lives of children, families, grassroots people, students, stakeholders, agencies, and collaterals. This book will help guide policy decisions when changes are made to the child welfare system.

MESSAGE TO POLICYMAKERS BASED ON THE BOOK'S TABLE OF CONTENTS

As social workers, we became concerned by our observations as we worked within the child welfare system. For example, the majority of children exiting the child welfare system graduate to other systems, including prison, welfare, and homelessness. We hope that as we zoom in the social justice lens to focus on the system, it will encourage our policymakers to address the issues that threaten the future of our country's children.

Throughout our years in this field of work, we have endeavored to prevent sexual violence, addictions, and domestic violence (SAD) from affecting children. We therefore look at the root causes by reviewing child welfare in the past and tracking how it has evolved into what it is today. We acknowledge that as the SAD pandemic continues over the years, it produces negative effects on our society. Many of the children and families affected by the SAD pandemic end up within the child welfare system—a system that has decayed over time and is now in need of some type of reform that will bring about positive changes and outcomes for children and families.

Similar to medical scientists, social workers are social scientists. We therefore must first find a diagnosis before we can treat the problem and bring healing and restoration. In order to diagnose, we will focus on the systemic issues/symptoms that cause problems in this village that has the responsibility to help raise its children. We will examine some of the things that happen within the child welfare village when children enter the system and some of the challenges they face when the system prepares them to leave the village, when they reach their age of majority. We will take a social justice perspective to advocate on their behalf.

We will then zoom out the social justice lens to view the different systems that interact and interconnect with the child welfare system. We know that a system does not exist on its own but that it is influenced and affected by the systems with which it interconnects and interacts.

Looking at the broader picture, our children interact with many other systems during their time in the child welfare system, and afterwards, some move directly into other systems or access resources that other systems provide. The impact of the SAD pandemic often continues to linger and results in our children transitioning into social systems such as the prison system and Employment and Income Assistance (EIA), thus continuing the cycle of dependency.

We hope that after the problem receives a proper diagnosis, we can join forces with policymakers and other stakeholders

MESSAGE TO POLICYMAKERS BASED ON THE BOOK'S TABLE OF CONTENTS

to combat the spread of the SAD pandemic. We can do this by looking at best practices that have worked in the past and applying these treatments/cures to see if they can successfully address the symptoms of SAD. And, as it has been said that there are no hopeless cases, only hopeless methods, we can also consider discontinuing remedies/strategies that have not worked in the past—especially if they have had an adverse effect. This change may call for different decisions; however, positive change never occurs without difficult decisions which may at times reject the status quo.

For the sake of accountability, we would then need to ensure that treatments for the SAD pandemic have a positive effect. Hence, we would need to conduct post-treatment reviews in order to determine what we should discontinue and discard, what we should recycle, and what we should change in order to reduce or end the spread of this pandemic. We will then be able to work collaboratively to make other recommendations that will bring about positive changes and outcomes for children and families who benefit from the services of the child welfare system.

ACKNOWLEDGMENTS

Many people have inspired and taught us; therefore, we would like to use this opportunity to pay our sincere respect and gratitude to the people who have made the writing of this book possible. Thanks to those who played an instrumental role in our upbringing during our early years, both in our immediate and extended families and in the communities and villages that raised us up on good morals and values. We thank our lovely families for their unconditional love and support.

We also thank those who have influenced our success in our careers as helping professionals: our formal and informal teachers who gave us the tools, including our university professors both in our home countries and at the University of Manitoba, our home away from home. We would also like to thank the individuals who provided training to us both locally and internationally. They have made a tremendous investment in our professional education throughout our social work careers. Indeed, their investment has yielded great returns and has influenced us to make our impact on the world as we help to change the lives of children.

As we have walked along our career paths, we have been privileged to have executive directors, directors, supervisors, and colleagues who have fueled our passion to keep fighting the "good fight." We are grateful for the guidance they have provided while cheering us on so that we never gave up. If we had given up, we would not have gained the knowledge and experience necessary to write this book.

Lastly, but most importantly, we are forever humbled to have the privilege to serve the children, along with their biological and foster families, who have opened their lives to us as we have journeyed with them through the child welfare system. They have made as much of an impact on us as we have on them. Therefore, we dedicate this book to these children and their families.

We hope that the power of this ink will leave an indelible mark upon all the lives of the people who open their hearts and minds to what we have written on these pages. Thank you in advance for taking action to impact the lives of future generations.

INTRODUCTION

Social work is a *helping* profession built on values that propel social workers into action leading to social justice. It is these values that create the passion in social workers to become advocates on behalf of the vulnerable, marginalize, and helpless in society.

Making changes in the lives of individuals, families, and communities, in countries and the world at large, is the huge task that social workers endeavour to undertake on a daily basis. But, you see, creating positive change is very challenging because it is so difficult to accomplish. However, change is the only thing that is constant. Individuals, families, communities, and countries constantly change over time. Otherwise, they remain stagnant. A state of stagnancy would eventually lead to death and decay, and no one wants themselves, or their family, community, or country to end up in a state of decay. Change is therefore inevitable for growth and prosperity.

Out of a desire for change, the authors of this book ventured out of their comfort zones, leaving behind their families, communities, and countries to embark on a journey to become "strangers in a foreign land." Though from different countries, what they had in common that attracted them to the *helping* profession and to this book project were some core values: (1) "Love thy neighbour as thyself," and (2) "Seek justice, love mercy, and walk humbly." These core values they were raised on also underpin the profession of social work.

It is no mere coincidence, then, that the authors would all end up in the same country, studying together at the same university in the same courses, and working in the same field. It seems as if they were destined to be Wonder Women who would join forces to help save the children entangled in a child welfare system where much social action is needed to bring about social change. They collaborated in order for children and families to receive social justice.

The challenging thing about change is that even though it is constant, it is very hard to accept, let alone implement, especially when it relates to making positive changes to large systems that affect the lives of individuals, families, communities, and countries. Whether systems thrive or decay, we all know that change is necessary for growth. While we do not have the power to speed up the process of change, we do have the "power of the pen," so we hope to use this superpower to help save the children. A social worker, like every other person in society, knows that children are the future. If the future gets entangled in a system that needs much-desired changes, then the future is at risk.

This worry, along with the desire to see social action, positive social change, and social justice, motivated the authors to write this book in order to be a voice for the voiceless and change agents for children. Empowered by twenty-five cumulative years of formal and on-the-job training and experience

Introduction

in the field of child welfare, we stand firmly on our social work values and ethics and are propelled by our hearts' desire to fight for social justice. We strive to make our impact on the changes that are looming over the child welfare system in the provinces and territories of Canada—a country that has become our home away from home. Looking through a social justice lens, this book is entitled *Child and Family Dis-services: Objective Perspective Inside the System*

List of Abbreviations

ADHD: Attention Deficit Hyperactivity Disorder
AFM: Addictions Foundation of Manitoba
BHF: Behavioural Health Foundation
CFS: Child and Family Services
CIC: Child in Care
CLDS: Community Living disABILITY Services
CSU: Crisis Stabilization Unit
EIA: Employment and Income Assistance
FASD: Fetal Alcohol Spectrum Disorder
IRAP: Individual Rate Adjustment Protocol
IQ: Intelligence Quotient
JOY: Just Organize Yourself
MATC: Manitoba Adolescent Treatment Centre
SAD: Sexual Violence, Addictions, and Domestic Violence
SNA: Service Needs Agreements
YASU: Youth Addictions Stabilization Unit

List of Editors and Contributors

Editor
Marci Rae Johnson

Contributors
Ithan Bullard PhD student,
MSW, RSW, MHT ....Endorsement

Pastor Dr. Brian Archer, PhD, P.Eng..............Endorsement

Dr. Aisha Tosan, DBA, MSc, PhD ....Endorsement
Executive Director, Bi-Communications,
Presenter, Crime Fighters

Kristy Sutton .... Letter to the Social Worker

Back cover professional photos ....Brittney Neubauer

PART ONE
RE-FORMED CHILD WELFARE

In this section, we will take you on a historical journey that shows how the need for protecting children from atrocities committed by their families and communities gave rise to the forming and reforming of laws and policies to protect their best interests. In addition, you will get a clear understanding of how the attempts to save children result in their entrance into a child welfare system.

ONE
CHILD WELFARE PAST AND PRESENT

IN THE BEGINNING of our journey as social workers, we learned the history of how the child welfare system began. In this book, we do not intend to give you this lecture, as we do not want you to wander off into slumber-land. However, while most people know children are precious gifts and believe we are all responsible to ensure that decisions are made in their best interests, you might be extremely surprised, if not disturbed, to know some of the things children have undergone in the past. Without looking into the past, we might not be able to understand why things are the way they are now. We will therefore provide you with a brief blast from the past in a snapshot.

Era	Child and Family Laws
BC- (Before Christ)	Egyptian *Book of the Dead*, Hammurabi Code, Mosaic Law, the Golden Age of Greece
AD- (In the year of our Lord)	Roman civilization, Visigothic Code, English law, Elizabethan Poor Law
	Early American law, twentieth century: 1950s, 1960s, 1970s

Table: A Child Welfare Values and Principles Put into Practice from Ancient Egypt to the Twenty-First Century, August 2004.

Follow along with us as we take you through Table A to provide insights into child welfare practices from past to present. Even in ancient times, people had a vested interest in the welfare of children. Cultural practices of social justice and altruism towards children were evident in portions of Northern Africa. The ancient Egyptians believed it was so important to protect children that they included a clause in their *Book of the Dead* which said that anyone who harmed or exploited children would be judged harshly on judgment day (Rycus and Hughes 1998, 3).

It is, however, heart-wrenching to know that during the BC era, other laws such as the Hammurabi Code in Babylon gave parents the right to see their children as what can be referred to as "cash cows." Sadly, the Hammurabi Code viewed the parent-child relationship as one of proprietary interest, and this practice of selling children continued in various legal codes for more than 3,000 years. Laws viewed children as economic units, so their parents could choose whether they wanted to sell or exchange them just as they would trade goods. Parents could even abuse, kill, or dismember their children without state interference. (Rycus and Hughes 1998, 3).

The Mosaic Law fully supported the concepts of the Hammurabi Code in addition to stating that children were expected to respect their parents. Hebrew society during this time used the books of the Bible as a rule of law, quoting scriptures contained in the book of Exodus to support their decisions. Exodus outlines rights and responsibilities of children and parents, as well as some of the consequences if these were not obeyed (Rycus and Hughes 1998, 3).

Towards the end of the BC era, during the Golden Age of Greece, Greek law made the practice of child maltreatment less permissible. Unlike the Hammurabi Code and Mosaic Law, Greek law did not allow parents to take their children's lives—they could only physically "chastise" the child. (Rycus and Hughes 1998,4).

Going into the AD period, during the era of Roman civilization society moved away from previous practices of selling and killing children. However, the father continued as the head of the home, ruling over his household until he died. This cultural practice shows that parents' rights continued to overrule the rights of children (Rycus and Hughes 1998, 4). The Visigothic Code, on the other hand, stressed the responsibilities of parents rather than their power. Under the Visigothic Code, "children could be punished or disinherited, but they could not be put to death or mutilated, and the sale of children was forbidden. Parents were given authority to use reasonable physical discipline but were not permitted to exceed what was considered reasonable" (Rycus and Hughes 1998, 5).

Toward the middle of the AD era, English law focused more on the rights of children instead of the previously mentioned laws that focused on the rights of parents. English law stated that:

- Children had rights and interests separate from others, including their parents.

- Parental rights were contingent rights (i.e., rights that were contingent upon the parent providing minimal care and nurturance and a home free of abuse).

- The state was the guarantor of that trust, responsible for intervening, when necessary, to protect children (Rycus and Hughes 1998, 5).

The practice of the state caring for children started at the beginning of the seventeenth century in England and Wales with the implementation of the Elizabethan Poor Law in 1601. This law was introduced due to extreme poverty at the time and intended to assist children who came from poor families. Even though the law was meant for good, more children ended up in state care under this law instead of as the responsibility of their community members. In the midst of wide-ranging corruption, resources were in many cases mis-directed, and a mere fraction of what was meant to be used to help the children actually got to them. Sad commentaries on abuse that occurred in the British welfare system during that era can be found in Charles Dickens' book *Oliver Twist*. The scarcity of resources made continuing the administration of the Elizabethan Poor Law impossible, so the government repealed the law in the mid-1600s. (Rycus and Hughes 1998,6).

Prior to the twentieth century, early American law emerged, modeling that of the Elizabethan Poor Law, and children's rights were not acknowledged. A reversion to the BC period when the Hammurabi Code was in effect occurred. The responsibility of caring for children again belonged to families and communities, and parents again could put their children to death if they were old enough to understand right from wrong but were being stubborn. With the passing of the Stubborn Child Act in 1628, parents regained the power to kill their children, and there was little-to-no protection against parents treating children cruelly or economically depriving them. (Rycus and Hughes 1998,6).

Now we will look at more familiar child welfare practices that occurred across North America going into the twenty-first century. The removal of children from their homes started as early as the period of the Elizabethan Poor Law which was later adopted by the Americans when the English settlers came. This included removing children from their family homes and placing them into alternative living situations. This need arose in the nineteenth century when many immigrant children became orphaned or were in need of protection due to the outbreak of diseases. In addition, the Indian Wars displaced many Native American families. The government placed orphaned or abandoned children during this time into almshouses. Then, toward the end of the nineteenth century, protecting children became more formalized with the founding of the first formal organization in 1874, named The Society for the Prevention of Cruelty to Children (SPCC). This organization in New York City was created by concerned citizens who were aware of the abuse of a child named Mary Ellen (Rycus and Hughes 1998, 8).

In the twentieth century, the American government passed laws to punish parents who neglected and/or were cruel to their children. Also, placing children in more stable and safe homes became the norm of the day. This new way of looking at child welfare was shaped from initiatives that considered homebased care versus placements. (Rycus and Hughes 1998, 8). Even to date in the twenty-first century, debates continue about whether or not customary care should take priority over stranger-based, out-of-home placements.

North American countries such as the United States and Canada modeled their child welfare practices similarly to those of the British. This included placing children in poor houses if they were from families that were poverty stricken or if they became orphaned.

Rycus and Hughes, in their paper titled "Child Welfare: Values and Principles Put into Practice: From Ancient Egypt to the Twenty-First Century" explained that in the early 1900s, children were rescued from poor houses and mental institutions that had deplorable conditions and were placed in institutional care such as orphanages or "children's homes." Child welfare policies were a response to the demonstratable terrible conditions that prevailed in many of the poor houses and mental institutions. In the early part of the twentieth century, starting in the 1920s, the introduction of the social work profession streamlined the field of child welfare and the child protection casework model in hopes of bringing about needed social change. In the 1950s, professionals began to recognize that family settings could better meet the needs of children than institutions, and the foster family home began to replace the orphanage as the primary child placement resource.

In the United States during the early 1970s, permanency planning and mandated reporting was legislated. If individual citizens and professionals suspected child maltreatment, they were obligated to report it. "This led to the dramatic increases in the number of investigations and in the number of children and families served in the child welfare system. It created an inevitable system overload that persisted in the child welfare field today". (Rycus and Hughes 1998, 10). However, in Canada, in practice, permanency planning had already come to be realized as important by the 1960s but mandatory reporting was implemented in the 1970s.

Let all that information settle in for a bit. Are you ready to look at what our children face in the present-day, twenty-first century child welfare system? As we mentioned in the introduction, change is constant. But if we take a close look at the past and compare it to the present practice of child welfare in Canada, can we identify some similar trends? And also, we need to analyze whether we actually provide a service or a **dis-service** to children and their families.

Revelations from the past will help give us a better understanding of the present situation as it relates to child welfare in Canada. Using the analogy of a **system** and the medical metaphor of a **pandemic,** the authors will take you through a process beginning from the root causes and ending with possible diagnosis and proposed treatment of systemic issues that have caused many children and families to be affected by SAD inter-generationally.

Dis-service: "to do something that hinders or is detrimental to one" (The Free Dictionary).

System: "A set of things working together as parts of a mechanism or an interconnecting network" (Dictionary.com).

Pandemic: (of a disease) "prevalent throughout an entire country, continent, or the whole world; epidemic over a large area" (Dictionary.com).

Era	Child and Family Laws Used in Canada
BC: before colonization	Villages raising children in communities
Post-colonization	• Newfoundland and Labrador Child, Youth and Family Services • Manitoba Child and Family Services Act and The Child and Family Services Authorities Act • British Columbia Child, Family and Community Service Act • New Brunswick Family Services Act • Alberta Child, Youth and Family Enhancement Act • Saskatchewan Child and Family Services Act • Ontario Child and Family Services Act • Quebec Youth Protection Act • Nova Scotia Child and Family Services Act • Prince Edward Island Child Protection Act • Yukon Child and Family Services Act

Table: B

Extract from the International Indigenous Policy Journal April 2013, Vol.4 Issue 2

Table B, above, illustrates the Canadian Provinces and the child welfare laws that came about post-colonization. Another important aspect of the contents of table B , is that , since June 1, 2017Ontario CFS has been governed by the provisions of its Child, Youth, and family services Act.

Now let us journey inside a twenty-first century child welfare system. Yes, in this present day and age, in our very own home and native land, we are still working on changing the laws and practices affecting our children and families since **colonization.** Over the decades, the different Canadian provinces have created many laws that govern the child welfare system. In Canada, the provinces have different names for services they offer to children and their families. For example, in Manitoba, it is called Child and Family Services and in some other provinces such as British Columbia, it is called Child Protective Services.

> **Colonization** is "the act of setting up a colony away from one's place of origin. ... With humans, colonization is sometimes seen as a negative act because it tends to involve an invading culture establishing political control over an indigenous population (the people living there before the arrival of the settlers)" (Vocabulary.com).

Colonization and Its Impact on Child Welfare in Canada

The village raised the children before the introduction of colonization. Did children in Canada need protection? Or did the need for protecting children arise due to how colonization created a **SAD pandemic**?

Did our present child welfare practices stem from the colonial past and its lasting impact on the social, psychological, and economic health of Canadian Society? Many of the children in the Canadian child welfare systems are affected by historical trauma and their parents' struggles with sexual violence, addictions, and domestic violence **(SAD).**

SAD: a systemic issue that affects the most vulnerable people of our society.		
Sexual Violence	Addictions	Domestic Violence
"Sexual harassment, sexual abuse, sexual exploitation, and unwanted sexting"	Alcohol, drugs, gambling	Domestic violence is "the power misused by one adult in a relationship to control another. It is the establishment of control and fear in a relationship through violence and other forms of abuse. This violence can take the form of physical assault, psychological abuse, social abuse, financial abuse, or sexual assault. The frequency of the violence can be on and off, occasional or chronic" (https://www.ncbi.nlm.nih.gov/pmc/articles/PMC2784629/).

Table: C

The table illustrates the authors' interpretation of the SAD pandemic collated from observation and experiences from working in the child welfare system.

What we now witness in Canadian society is a modernized system based upon legislations that disempowered families and communities from their traditional roles of raising children. Based on conversations with various individuals during field placement, the majority shared the view that colonization impacted their traditional roles of raising children. They felt that their cultural practices of childrearing were invaded. Looking through a social justice lens, the authors will help magnify the intricate details and bring clarity on the system's operations. Many share the view that the child welfare system has not really changed from its colonial past. We are therefore left to wonder if the system is providing dis-services to children and families.

In Chapter 2, we will look at how children and families enter the child welfare system as a result of the intergenerational spread of the SAD pandemic. However, before moving forward into the present, we will zoom in on some of the past child welfare situations we previously mentioned and compare those to what currently happens to our children.

Let us take you back to ancient Roman civilization. During this period, people practiced the sale, mutilation, or killing of children and viewed children as property. Have these practices changed in the twenty-first century?

The current child welfare system shows some similarities when children end up with a price tag placed upon their heads—especially when provincial or federal funding models rate and fund them, causing potential caregivers to see them as a "priced" possession. For example, one caregiver once introduced his foster child as "my $100 child" to his friends while making fun of the child welfare system. Does the child welfare system offer these children a dis-service by using language that depicts cash for care and allowing people to view the process of caring for children as a "cash for kids" exchange? Have we really moved away from these negative practices of the past?

Also, there has been a constant increase in the number of children who enter the child welfare system, which can be compared to the increase in the number of children who needed the services with the introduction of the Elizabethan Poor Laws. Within modern-day Canadian society, we are reforming laws to address the increase in the number of children entering the child welfare system. This is like what happened when the Elizabethan Poor Law was repealed. Later in the book, in Chapter 6, we will provide data which shows a correlation between the implementation of the Child and Family Services Authorities Act in Manitoba and increase number of children in the child welfare system. The numbers has doubled since the introduction of the Child and Family Services Authorities Act in Manitoba in 2003. Similar to the Elizabethan Poor Law, the Child and Family Authorities Act was intended for good. Instead, a system dependency syndrome occurred that resulted in an increased burden on child welfare system spending, so much so that the government had to move into new funding models in order to curb the influx of children into the system—just as how the Elizabethan Poor Law was repealed when there was a scarcity of resources and it became a burden to the government at that time. What can we learn from the past? Have there been any serious attempts to learn from the past and change current child welfare practices?

As social workers, we recognize that change usually takes place in phases and stages and that over time change occurs in cycles. We also are aware that change moves from micro, to mezzo, to macro levels. At the micro level, in the family system, some children have already been exposed to the SAD pandemic within their homes, while others are exposed in utero from the use of drugs and alcohol during pregnancy. They have already experienced trauma in utero from domestic violence.

On the mezzo level, the child welfare system removes children from their home environments to another system in order to protect them from the symptoms of SAD. Children experience both positive and negative situations during their transition from their home environments and adjustment to this bigger system.

Macro-level policymakers at the community, agency, and government levels make decisions to protect children in environments free from the SAD pandemic. As we examine the effects and magnitude of the SAD pandemic, we will explore the effects of other macro-level systems and their decisions. Is the CFS system the only system that can deal with the SAD pandemic? Should other interrelated systems work cooperatively together at the mezzo level to combat the pandemic?

We do not expect that simply advocating for change means that change will happen. But we must take social action in hopes that the desired systemic changes will eventually come. Will it ever be possible for us to go back to the good old days where the village raised the child? Or will we continue to allow children affected by the SAD pandemic to be fed into the current child welfare system and then eventually transition into other systems? In the next chapter, we will demonstrate how children enter the child welfare system and what happens to them while they are in the system.

TWO
ENTERING THE SYSTEM

Entering the System

TO GET A clearer understanding of why our children end up in the child welfare system, let us enlighten you on the SAD pandemic. Unless you can visualize the process, it is difficult to grasp this present reality and its root causes. As one mother stated, "I grew up seeing my mom taking cocaine and my dad with the brown paper bag every day at his head." The SAD pandemic is real. It is the reality of today's generation, and the SAD pandemic isn't just a pandemic; it's a cycle. We see a mother who is a product of the Child and Family Services (CFS) system, whose child is now being apprehended, as she looks at the worker and shouts, "When will it end? Who will end it?" This is the story of many parents of children whose lives are touched by the child welfare system.

Sexual violence, addictions, and domestic violence (SAD) had its incubation during the post-colonial period in Canada. This pandemic is a man-made problem that developed because of the post-traumatic effects of colonization. Sexual abuse was rampant, and some children who suffered this atrocity grew up and continued the cycle against their own children, or they buried their trauma with drugs and alcohol. The SAD pandemic kept spreading as it passed from generation to generation. As children were born into families affected by this pandemic, the need for protecting and saving them arose. Thus, laws were passed to offer protective services to children who had been impacted by the SAD pandemic, and the court decides if children need temporary or permanent protection from their home environments.

These laws place the onus on the public. Whenever someone notices a possible SAD situation, they have a legal responsibility to report it to the authorities. When a member of a community can see that a home has the smoke of abuse, neglect, domestic violence, and addiction rising through its chimney and polluting the atmosphere of social norms, then they know they should call CFS.

CFS then removes children from unsafe home environments and provides treatment so that the SAD pandemic does not continue to infect their lives. Additionally, if parents expecting a baby refuse to address their struggle with the SAD pandemic or to provide an alternative caregiver, professionals must ensure that hospitals do not discharge newborns into homes infected with the SAD pandemic.

In the best interests of vulnerable newborns, child and family service agencies must issue a birth alert to hospitals directing them to notify CFS when parents give birth to such a child. These children enter the child welfare system as soon as they make their grand entrance into the world. Their CFS "superhero" will come to their "rescue" and deliver them to homes which they hope SAD has not infected.

Of note, there was an infamous case of physical abuse in North America in the last year of the twentieth century which involved a prominent, wealthy New York City lawyer convicted of murdering his foster daughter. Since then, the Canadian public has learned that even trusted and respected community members like doctors, teachers, and priests can inflict sexual abuse (Bala et al. 2004, 23). Therefore, when CFS removes children from homes infected by SAD and places them in perceived "safer homes," do we really solve the problem?

Certainly, we must accept that child abuse and neglect can happen in any part of the world, among people of any social group, race, religious belief, or social status. With this being said, we would like to emphasize that the Canadian child welfare system also includes immigrant children, though at a lower percentage. Cultural differences in gender roles in some countries result in the social acceptance of physical discipline and domestic violence towards women and children, and these practices are not considered illegal in some African and Middle Eastern countries. As a result, when some families migrate to Canada, they continue these cultural practices, unaware that they are illegal in modern-day North American societies. In Canada, these acts are punishable by law, as there is a zero-tolerance policy towards domestic violence. Some immigrant families therefore lose their children to the child welfare system because of their cultural practices.

Additionally, some families that have migrated to Canada originate from places where children are safe in their villages. They therefore allow children under the age of twelve to freely roam the streets of their village without any direct adult supervision. Many of these cultures also expect that all the adults in the community will look out for the safety of the children. Parents in these cultures do not view it as abandonment or neglect if they allow their children under twelve to stay home alone while they go out to work or run errands. These families, when they move to Canada, must become acculturated into Canadian society regarding child safety practices. Based on these types of unintentional acts of omission, a member of the public may sound the alarm for CFS intervention in the lives of these families.

Some immigrant families are also not aware that children who get pregnant under the age of eighteen may trigger CFS involvement. Therefore, a child can be born wearing a CFS label because its parents have not reached the legal age of adulthood, as CFS believes children of underage parents are at high risk.

Ignorance of the law is not considered a viable excuse. However, as frontline workers, over the past 10 years we have discovered that many communities, individuals, and parents are unaware of laws, policies and procedures when their families come under the radar of the child welfare system and the consequences of it. For example, there are public awareness campaign ads on TV about how we should treat animals, but there are none focused on how we should treat children.

When there is a child maltreatment investigation, many parents are quick to ask the question, "why are you taking my kids?" But if their pets were taken, they would understand that they had done something wrong and they would not ask such a question. And many Canadian parents are aware of the existence of a Child Tax Credit but are ignorant of the laws concerning child protection. We have continually pushed the blame to others without thoroughly using the justice lens to examine ourselves. Would fewer children end up in CFS if individuals, communities, and parents were fully aware of the child welfare act and of their own responsibilities?

Now that we have shed some light on the situation and magnified it, we hope you have a very clear understanding of how children enter the child welfare system. Let us turn now to the effects of the pandemic.

From a social justice perspective, the first agent of socialization for a human being is within a family system. This system provides an atmosphere where children learn the language and traditions of their culture. It is where they first build stable relationships and learn positive social norms. If this system is essential to building the foundation for children, it follows that we would make every effort to preserve the family system and make it a healthy unit where children could flourish and thrive. Somehow, though, it seems that as a society we either minimize or refuse to accept the fact that the SAD pandemic prevents some individuals from carrying out their duties as parents.

In Canadian history, colonization influenced a pandemic that threatens the health of many families. The family system started decaying as a result of the removal of a critical component: the nucleus of the system. When children were removed from their families to be raised in institutions, it affected their physical, mental, emotional, and spiritual health, which resulted in trauma. Most of the parents who suffered from the SAD pandemic abandoned and abused their children, which left their children in need of care and protection. This pandemic did not stop its spread but has affected their children and their children's children for generations, as over time, post-traumatic stress results in poor coping strategies such as addictions to substances.

SAD affected families seek treatment or a cure in hope that they will recover and that the family will be restored. During this process, however, the children need to be removed and placed with another family or in residential facilities that re-socialize them. The children now become part of a new system, CFS. In the next chapter, we will zoom in the lens on the CFS system and provide a clear understanding of what happens to children who end up within this system after their removal from their families.

PART TWO
VILLAINY IN THE VILLAGE

Villainy in the village first shows itself when children are younger and are subtly used during the cash for care exchange. We notice this phase when children first enter the child welfare system. As they get older and prepare to exit the child welfare system, some are further exploited for cash as they are used to make money for the "johns" and drug dealers who see them as a commodity for these lucrative businesses.

The phrase, "it takes a village to raise a child" applies universally.

> It Takes a Village to Raise a Child

This phrase has no racial or cultural boundaries. As children, we were very fortunate to experience the love and support of the villagers in the African and Caribbean communities where we were raised. It was the norm for many aunties, uncles, grandmas and grandpas, godmothers and godfathers, neighbours, and other community members to care for us and raise us. We often hear that it takes cash to care, but this was not a reality for many of us who grew up in communities where cash was scarce. People cared for children naturally and without reservation; everyone who had genuine love for them would willingly use portions of what they had earned to meet the children's needs. The people in our village invested whatever little cash they had in the future of the children.

If a child needed care and protection, an aunt, uncle, grandma, grandpa, godmother, godfather, neighbour, or church member would rise to the occasion and protect the precious gift. They would care for and nurture the child and guide him or her until the child was old enough to go out and face the world. As the child grew, the community would help him or her receive a good education or begin a trade so that they could become a successful adult, able to earn a living for themselves.

We ourselves are products of villages who celebrated our success and were proud to reap the returns on their investments. Not only that, but having the opportunity to venture out of our communities to make our impact abroad in a foreign land is the kind of accomplishment that our families and village members wanted for us. They helped equip us to face the "new world" on a different continent in a first world country.

It was a revelation and a culture shock when we encountered a village that has a "system" to raise children. Even more interesting, this "system" is one where children receive care based on the amount of cash attached to them. While we understand that it takes cash to care, it is ironic when we compare our experiences in our villages and realize that people who genuinely care for children have no problem using their own cash to take care of children in need.

One of the major challenges we face is trying to acculturate ourselves into a value system that focuses more on cash to care for the child. We have come to realize that what matters most in this system is not valuing children for who they are and what we want them to become for the future. As we also look through a social justice lens, this is something we have struggled to accept. There seems to be a shift of focus in the social aspect as it relates to how we communicate about providing care for our children. The emphasis seems to be more on the cost to care as we negotiate financials and exchange cash for care. Is there a need for a paradigm shift?

Is it possible to have conversations where we encourage family and community members to be more open to the idea of the village raising the child, instead of encouraging extended family members and caregivers to decide whether or not children are "worth enough" to receive the love and care they deserve? During these conversations, we need to explain that the children are by-products of the SAD pandemic and have become very vulnerable and helpless. The children have no control over SAD impacting their parents' lives, yet they must deal with the consequences that SAD brings. One of the side effects of the SAD pandemic is that children end up in the child welfare system.

THREE
CASH FOR CARE

What happens within the Child and Family Services system?

"The Auction"—Cash for kids exchange

Child and Family Dis-services

WE ACKNOWLEDGE THAT it is costly to raise children. To this end, the government of Canada allows families to benefit from the Child Tax Credit to assist with offsetting some of the expenses incurred in the raising of children. But are we doing a dis-service to children when they end up in a situation were more monetary incentives are given when they enter the child welfare system? When did it become socially acceptable to have a casual conversation in public encouraging someone to foster children so they can get a certain amount of extra, tax-free cash? It is very shocking to know that people can have these types of conversations without reservations. Have we lost our ethical integrity as it relates to how we value our children? Should a child's monetary value be the main incentive for a caregiver's willingness to take care of children?

This sometimes creates a situation in which children seem to be auctioned off. As social workers, we often feel pressured to embellish our writing in order to convince our funders of what our children are worth. We have policies and protocols we must follow in order to rate children according to how much their caregivers should be paid. Using a pen instead of a microphone to echo our voices, we speak loudly to the holders of the moneybag. We are encouraged to swindle them into paying high prices for our children. Whether we request the money through Service Needs Agreements (SNA), Individual Rate Adjustment Protocol (IRAP), Level 5 Funding, or just request a basic rate, we hope to get the price we ask for.

We also hope our auction is successful because we fear being unable to find caregivers willing to take children unless a good price is offered.

It is heartrending to discover that sometimes a child who needs protection from suspected abusers doesn't get the opportunity to live in a safer environment because the asking rate is denied. It is even more disappointing when a child doesn't get the chance to live in a safe home in a kinship care setting because the demand that the family made was not approved. Sometimes if the cash for care exchange rate was unsuccessful, it leaves a child without the opportunity to live with a family.

We have shifted our focus from how much we value a child to what the price value of a child is. This therefore begs the question: Are we making placement decisions in the best interests of children, or do we make decisions based on the children who bring in the best "interest"? Do the children who bring in the best "interest" drive caregivers' decisions to love and care for them? Children who bring in the best "interest" are those who have the big labels such as Fetal Alcohol Spectrum Disorder (FASD) or Attention Deficit Hyperactivity Disorder (ADHD), or have high behavioral needs and are scored at level five. Some of these children, when placed in specialized homes, require high monetary compensation because these issues come with increased costs such as counseling services, special care for high medical needs, etc.

Sometimes, when there is a "silent auction," where a child's behaviors and needs are on display for all to see but they haven't had a professional assessment for learning disabilities and mental health challenges, they have no bidders. Without a formal diagnosis, their worth decreases. Formally diagnosed children have a very high price tag, so they are more likely to find a home. Many homes create "specialized placement" for children with special labels and high price tags. But are the children receiving the specialized care they need?

Based on the foregoing information, some people genuinely care about the wellbeing of children, while others provide care to children as a lucrative business. When does caring for children become income instead of a genuine interest in the wellbeing of children? Caring for children can become an attractive package deal without taxes. From a social justice lens, we can view this kind of operation as a villainous act.

If there is villainy in the village, one is only left to ask the question, "who will save the children?"

Social Workers?

> **Villain:** "a villain is often defined by their acts of cruelty and cunning, and displays immoral behavior that can oppose or pervert justice. The antonym of a villain is a hero" (Wikipedia).

Our social work values often conflict with system expectations and demands. Imagine that you must choose the best placement for a child, and you hear the voice of the **villain** whispering in your ear, "I have a safe home where the child can be with her sibling but only on the basis that I receive a service fee of $X amount." You know it is ideal to place a child with the family, but you resist the temptation of buying into the villainous act of the cash for kids exchange. You refuse the offer, only to have the child stare you in the eyes, trying very hard to hold back the tears that are welling up in his/her innocent, dark brown eyes as they ask questions that you have grave trouble answering. "Why am I not allowed to live with my family?" "Where am I going to live?" "Do you know the people I am going to live with?"

In all honesty, you really do not know how to answer these questions because it might cause even greater emotional wounding to reveal the truth. If you were in this situation, what would you do? Would you make the decision in the best interest of the child, or would you offer the caregiver the "$X" amount of funds they have demanded?

When dealing with these types of value conflicts, social workers must choose their battles carefully. It is a real struggle when social workers desire to save children from homelessness but do not want to participate in the cash for kids exchange. When they are caught up in the middle of it all, social workers sometimes ask themselves the question, "How did I end up in this field of work?" and they have to be careful not to become one of the villains in the village.

The impact of wearing a CFS label is that families often view social workers as the enemy instead of the hero. This hinders the service users from tapping into the skills, knowledge, and expertise that trained and licensed social work professionals bring to them. Our social work values and ethics, which include being non-judgmental and anti-oppressive, meeting individuals where they are at, and building on their strengths, often remain unseen. Instead, we are usually seen as villains who destroy families. The social work profession is sometimes buried under labels such as "protection worker," "family service worker," "direct service worker," "my worker," and other titles that are not a true reflection of what the social work profession entails and what our roles should be.

Yet, despite the many challenges we face in our efforts to save the children, social workers keep on fighting the good fight. There are many battles fought and victories won on behalf of children and their families. It is by no means an easy task to equip oneself with social work values and ethics while entangled in a disempowering system, but most social workers choose to rise above the odds and stand up for social justice. Even though they might not be seen as superheroes, they make the decision to take action to bring about positive change in the lives of children and their families.

In order to provide services to children and families, social workers must grapple with some realities that are counterproductive to this effort, such as the cash for kids' example above. These realities make the task of saving children very daunting. You might therefore ask the question, why do they even bother to fight for social justice when all the odds show it might be a losing battle? What are the odds working against the children and their families? To have a clear picture of this situation, we will properly analyze the battlefield. Every superhero must be strategic prior to venturing into the battlefield.

Social workers do not have superpowers and have to rely only on their theoretical, evidence-based practice, and practical knowledge if they are to succeed in their interventions. Such interventions are carried out at various levels: micro, mezzo, and macro. Change then follows suit.

The Micro, Mezzo, and Macro Level Systems of Intervention

Systems Diagram

The Systems Diagram shows various levels of the system. At the core of the diagram, children and families represent the micro level system. Social workers have to navigate all of these systems at the various levels in order to advocate for children and their families. Why do social workers have to advocate? Unfortunately, it is because every system exposes children to some level of villainy. This can manifest in many different shapes and forms. Some acts might be more subtle and go unnoticed, while other acts are frightening and threaten the safety and well-being of children.

On the micro level, children experience the SAD pandemic in their homes. This necessitates social work intervention, and their superhero comes in to rescue them. In this micro-level system, the villains are often the parents and relatives of the children, so social workers often ask the question: "are the villagers their own worst enemies?" As superheroes, we often must go on rescue missions where the smoke of the SAD pandemic billows from a home.

To envision situations like this more clearly, imagine you must go into a home to intervene and save the children. Upon doing your investigation, you realize that, on this day, the family had received its child tax credits, and they kept the children home from school. The children then witnessed their mom and her boyfriend, as well as some relatives and their boyfriends, using substances, drinking, and fighting. The oldest child got scared and called 911. To further compound the situation, during your interview, one child disclosed that her mom's cousin had sexually assaulted her while he was under the influence of drugs and alcohol. Children need to be saved from these sad situations where the SAD pandemic has taken over their homes.

As you can see, the villains that social workers must battle in this case are the children's own family members. Even though it might be hard to accept, we must find a way to

Child and Family Dis-services

save children from families who have become their own worst enemies. For these and other reasons, families often view social workers as the enemy, and it makes our job very hard when we try to build relationships with families such as these. It is ironic that after doing an intervention in this situation, the "superheroes" are slapped with labels such as "home wreckers" and "family destroyers." In these situations, superheroes face a lot of rejection.

These are not the only kinds of battles these superheroes fight. The second layer of the systems diagram represents the mezzo-level systems. This brings even more challenges because the villains are more subtle when they carry out their villainous activities. Social workers entangled in these mezzo-level systems have to learn to play the game of the professional hypocrite in their struggle to navigate and network with collateral agencies. Some of the barriers they face are jurisdictional boundaries, discrimination, structural and cultural oppression, polite racism, and **crab barrel syndrome**.

> **Crab barrel syndrome** "is defined as early as the 20th century by Filipino feminist and activist Ninotchka Rosca. Here, one person may prosper in a specific community or ethnic group, but jealousy and self-loathing bring that person back to the level of the impoverished community". (Blackdiasporaaffais)

The superheroes who have intervened and removed children from their family villages will now have to navigate children in care (CIC) through various systems. This is not without its challenges because not only do the superheroes wear the CFS label but also CIC ends up getting a CFS label, and their CFS superhero becomes their "guardian." Social workers hope they can now put children into safer home environments, but they have little power and control over what happens to children when they encounter the other systems in the mezzo environment.

While social workers can save many children in the ways we have been discussing, many other children fall through the cracks because these heroes are so busy on the many rescue missions they have to attend to. These heroes are usually given assignments way above the twenty cases recommended by mezzo-level policymakers as outlined in the Phoenix Sinclair inquiry report in recommendation 12.1 (The Legacy of Phoenix Sinclair, Achieving the Best for All Our Children, Vol 2, Dec 2013, 379). In addition, recommendation 15.5 1a states that there should be funding to allow agencies to meet a caseloads ratio of twenty cases per worker for all family services worker (The Legacy of Phoenix Sinclair, Achieving the Best for All Our Children, Vol 2, Dec 2013, 396).

To save more children from dying at the hands of the villains in their family villages, the government performs inquiries on high-profile child death cases. Despite the recommendations that came out of these inquiries, child welfare agencies place heavy burdens on the shoulders of the children's superheroes. How can these superheroes do justice for children when they are so overworked and burned out? Usually their assigned tasks become overwhelming after a very short period in the field. Oftentimes they bow out of this honorable service just when they are starting to build relationships with children and their families. This leads to high staff turnover rates and often incomplete rescue missions.

Children sometimes are left hanging in the balance while they wait for another superhero to pick up where their former superhero had left off. If social workers are so overworked that they can only focus on putting out fires as they pop up, it begs the question, again, "are we actually providing services or doing a dis-service to children and their families?"

Sadly, most of the time when villainous acts towards children go unattended, many of our children not only suffer, but they also end up falling through the cracks. This, then, requires the attention of macro-level system interventions. The Manitoba Advocate for Children and Youth, in their call to action for early intervention and prevention states: "We all share responsibility that there are peoples in our province and our country who continue to be ignored and disadvantaged by the structural barriers that have been established and reinforced because we do not unanimously demand their improvement" (2019, 55).

Social workers are not always able to successfully save children when agency leaders wear blinders that distract them from seeing their plight. This lack of vision prevents us from offering the best services to children and families.

Additionally, do we offer a dis-service to children and families when leaders sometimes choose workers based on nepotism rather than on the training, qualifications, and experience the job requires? When the system wounds heroes, it makes it even more difficult for them to save children when they go onto the battlefield. And in addition to these wounds the system inflicts, some of our superheroes experience vicarious trauma from exposure in the field.

Family drama, crises, and even physical and verbal attacks plague the battlefield, and these often wound superheroes during their combat missions. Sometimes these social workers end up working for child protection without the opportunity to have self-protection. When social workers get policies that encourage them to work alone in order not to drain limited staff resources, they must resort to calling the police for backup. Much to their dismay, though, the help is often slow in coming. These kinds of battles with subtle, systemic villainous acts work against the rescue mission. The heroes are left to wonder if the children will ever be saved.

Sometimes, however, superheroes can join forces with and find support from some of our concerned citizens who are sensitive to the plight of our children. For example, in the appendix to this book is one experience we had with a foster mother that shows what difference a social worker can make. Please see the appendix for a poem taken from a January 10, 2019 Facebook Social Work Tutor Letter to the Social Worker, written by Kristy Sutton.

Let us now look at the *post-rescue mission* to see what happens in the safer home environments in the CFS Village.

- **Kinship placements**

Generally, in Canada, the child welfare legislation of most provinces/territories encourages a "family first" approach in which a child's first placement option should be within their extended family or community. It is always a good feeling when extended family members open their doors to provide a safe place for children. The success rate for kinship placement is sometimes affected by the family's resistance to CFS involvement. Though sometimes hesitant because of the negative stigma that being involved with CFS brings to their home, some do say yes to CFS workers doing a safety check to assess their homes and to perform criminal background checks for approval to provide kinship care.

Instead of having CFS agency workers continue to show up on their doorsteps for an extended period, we sometimes encounter grandparents who prefer to have the privilege of guardianship of their vulnerable family members, be it their grandsons, granddaughters, grandnephews, or grandnieces. Some of these grandparents prove themselves the real heroes in these children's lives, as they are willing to help the children work through the post-traumatic SAD effects they have experienced.

As these grandparents attempt to get their grandchildren settled in their new homes and schools, they sometimes have to navigate systemic barriers. Because these children now wear a CFS label, there are special requirements that must be met when they enroll in schools, connect with community resources, and even when taking family vacations. These legalities sometimes do not work out in their favour. Grandparents can find the impediments of not being "a legal guardian" frustrating.

It is even more frustrating when grandparents have to fight against injustices towards their grandchildren, who sometimes have difficulty settling into their new homes, and as a result they act out. To further compound the situation, their grandchildren are sometimes treated as outcasts when they are too traumatized to quickly fit into new system expectations at school and in community resource programs. However, many grandparents refuse to give up. Some even go as far as securing their own lawyers and facing the courts. While some grandparents prove themselves so fit as it relates to the best interest of their grandchildren that the CFS agency support them by covering the legal cost of obtaining guardianship. They endure the legal process until they win the battle with the CFS agency and take over the coveted title of "legal guardian."

- **Alternative placements: when SAD impacts all family members and there is no suitable family to place the children with**

You may think it a bit far-fetched that everyone in a child's family could be impacted by the SAD pandemic in one way or another, yet this sometimes happens. This is a sad situation when you think of it. What do we do after searching through the child's genogram dating back to at least two generations, only to realize that the family's history of child welfare involvement goes back that far? The only solution is to find a safe, stranger-based home for the child.

While rescued children wait for their heroes to find suitable family placements for them, they sometimes get placed in group homes. And removing children from their homes does not mean they no longer experience the symptoms of SAD. When children suffer from the symptoms of SAD (whether from in-utero exposure or exposure in the home environment), they may experience developmental delays and display behavioral problems because of the trauma they have faced. They then need specialized placements to address these SAD symptoms. Therefore, they are placed in therapeutic foster care treatment homes.

Saving the children seems like an impossible mission, but we never lose faith that there is still hope. There is still hope if their heroes have expertise, if they are equipped with experiential knowledge, if they have social work background and training, if they are registered with a licensing regime that provides adequate procedural provision for social workers. If all these accountability measures are in place across the service delivery system, then we can celebrate many victories and share our stories of where justice has been served for children and their families. We hope to share these success stories of battles won in the second book of this series, *Child and Family Dis-services: Who Will Save the Children?*

FOUR
PREPARING TO EXIT THE SYSTEM

BELIEVE IT OR not, our children do grow up fast; as a matter of fact, they grow up too fast. Because of the SAD pandemic, growing up in the child welfare village comes with its own challenges. As we mentioned in Chapter 3, superheroes must help our children navigate various systemic barriers at different levels.

Nevertheless, as children get older, they enter a stage where they want to discover their own identity. At this stage in their development, they believe they can navigate and explore on their own. They sometimes resist the protection of social workers and caregivers, yet they are often confused and struggle with identity and self-esteem issues, and they are usually great risk takers. Little do they realize that the impact the SAD pandemic has on them makes them very vulnerable while they are preparing to transition out of the system. They now must battle with their personal demons as well as with the monsters and villains that lie in wait to take advantage of their vulnerability.

SAD takes on a new face as our children get older. Instead of only witnessing SAD, as was the case when they were younger, while they continue to be victims of SAD, many also become perpetrators, thus continuing the SAD cycle. The statistics are very alarming for the number of children in care who become victims of sexual exploitation or end up as addicts and/or in relationships plagued by domestic violence. Due to their vulnerability, "johns," drug dealers, and gang leaders/members may take advantage of them. These are now the monsters that superheroes must battle against while assisting with their preparations to transition out of care.

This period is known as the age of majority planning, which begins when the child turns fifteen. During this process, the assigned worker meets with the child and other collaterals to discuss how the child will exit the system. The worker will assess and review the child's file to determine whether the child has completed life skills training, either in school or at a day program. The life skills training ensures the child acquires basic life skills such as cooking, personal hygiene, financial management, employment searching, tenancy responsibilities, and housing rights knowledge.

In addition, the assigned worker must have the child complete a psychological evaluation which includes testing and assessment. This assessment determines the child's psychological and intellectual functioning. For example, if the child scores below seventy in the Intelligence Quotient (IQ) test, the social worker must refer the child to adult services for future support. Many children in care have an IQ below seventy, which is because of FASD and SAD.

School or trade participation/engagement is also part of age of majority planning. A child in care is expected to complete high school or trade school before exiting the child welfare system. However, many CIC struggle with this requirement.

During Transition

Reconnecting with family:

Lack of relationship due to removal from family in the formative years makes this connection difficult and increases a child's vulnerability when they exit care. Often, if they do end up connected with family, it happens only after spending months, if not years, couch surfing with different relatives in hopes of finding family they can get along with well enough to have a stable home, and sometimes reconnection with family may influence involvement in negative lifestyles. The quest to belong to a family sometimes leads to children finding solace in gangs, which may be the closest connection to what they believe is family. Also, gang membership is an alternative to becoming homeless, and they are already predisposed to homelessness on their journey of transitioning out of care.

In August 2017, the issue of youth ageing out of care and its correlation to homelessness was again brought to the forefront of public knowledge, which warranted an investigation. Thus, the Canadian Homelessness Research Network led by Dr. Stephen Gaetz released findings from a study they conducted that showed a link between the child welfare system and homelessness. This study found that almost two of every five of the study's participants confirmed they had "aged out" of provincial or territorial care. This statistic is alarming because past CFS respondents were 200 times more likely to become homeless than their counterparts in the general population who did not have CFS involvement (*CBC* August 9, 2017). What we see today is that some youths who have traumatic experiences often do not transition successfully into adults who can provide shelter for themselves.

Preparing for independent living:

Those who work cooperatively with the agency upon approaching their age of majority may explore independent living and get the opportunity to have their own place to call home. However, many take advantage of the freedoms that this age brings, which leads to negative consequences. Reaching the long-awaited and coveted "legal age" for drinking often leads to drinking parties, which in turn can lead to violent acts and police involvement.

Children who have aged out can often go into the community and do whatever they want without adult supervision. Sometimes they participate in criminal activities when they are out late at night. Freedom also increases their risk of experiencing sexual assault when they are out in bars or at social events. Drinking alcohol impairs their ability to make safe decisions, so they may end up leaving these events with random strangers. And then, some of our children never make it home and become a statistic on the missing persons list. It is alarming to know that Manitoba has the largest number of missing children in Canada. (A Place Where It Feels Like Home: The Story of Tina Fontaine 2019, 97).

Age of majority allowance:

After turning eighteen years old, children believe they are now adults, but with the impact of SAD and of childhood trauma, some of our children function way below the cognitive development milestones for their age. They lack the capacity to think rationally, reason, and problem solve. And now they must manage their own funds, since their caregivers no longer receive cash to provide care. Because of their low cognitive functioning, this sometimes leads to the use of these funds to feed their addictions and those of friends and relatives.

Challenges in transition: fighting the villains, personal demons, and monsters

Sexual violence, addictions, and domestic violence (SAD) are now carried out by villains such as "johns," drug dealers, boyfriends/girlfriends, parents, and other relatives who exploit our children. These monsters participate in the cash for kids exchange through sexual exploitation, pump their victims up with drugs and alcohol, and manipulate them so that they can take advantage of them. "It is a heartbreaking and desperate truth that here in Manitoba, adults actively lure, demand, and routinely purchase sex from children and youth, a crime that violates their human rights and dignity" (*A Place Where It Feels Like Home* 2019, 90). For example, sexually exploited youth demographics in Manitoba indicate that most youth are exploited by: a friend (34%), family member (20%), other/unknown (16%), boyfriend/girlfriend (11%), sexual offender (11%), drug dealer (5%), or gang member (3%) (*A Place Where It Feels Like Home* 2019, 91).

This kind of villainy often goes unnoticed because it has become a great profit-making business where children are traded for cash. As noted in the Tina Fontaine Report, in Manitoba, the Street Reach program's data from the last five years shows an average of 300 different children exploited in Winnipeg each year. Recall that, on average, $280,000 per year of illicit profit can be made per sexually exploited youth. Based on these figures (300 x $280,000), a low estimate would mean that an average of eighty-four million dollars a year flows into the hands of human traffickers, gangs, and drug dealers as a result of the commercial sexual exploitation of children and youth (2019, 105).

Instability and lack of income make these children vulnerable to exploitation, which sometimes takes the form of their use as drug mules. They may also decide to exchange sexual favours in order to satisfy their addictions, which sometimes leads to unplanned pregnancies. Pregnant teenagers are at increased risk of having a child that will end up in care of the child welfare system, thus continuing the SAD cycle. We will further explore this in Chapter 6, "The Cycle Continues."

In addition to suffering from the above villainous acts, children, when aging out of care, struggle with personal demons. Some of these demons they have to battle are addictions to street drugs, participation in gangs, peer pressure and negative peer influences, mental illness, FASD, low Intelligence Quotient (IQ), low self-esteem, frequent absenteeism from school, and lack of employability, just to name a few. When they lose the battle against these demons, they oftentimes end up in unhealthy relationships—sometimes having multiple partners as well as experiencing family violence.

A combination of these situations makes them lose trust in most individuals, whom they now see as monsters. They become so crippled with fear that they learn to accept these abnormalities as reality and put up resistance to accepting help, sometimes making statements such as, "it is in my family to drink, do drugs, and die." This leads to a journey towards dependence on other systems. How can we end this?

Our aim is to get parents, agencies, community leaders, both federal and provincial governments, business owners, and the public to work in partnership and take action. We must reflect on how significant our impact and influence are and the effects that our actions have on children. If we are not willing to take action at these various levels—micro, mezzo, and macro—not only will we provide dis-services to children in care, but we also fail to serve the future of our country. The children are the potential leaders of our country, and they are the ones who will sustain our legacy.

Fighting with these individuals, systems, and personal demons that work adversely against a smooth transition plan can sometimes feel like an uphill battle for workers. Ideally, in the "perfect" world of child welfare, workers hope to prepare the child to exit the system based on the guidelines laid out. Instead of having an ideal transition plan so they can transition into independence, however, these children end up transitioning into dependence on other systems in order to address the devastating side effects of SAD.

One of these systems is Employment and Income Assistance (EIA), since children affected by SAD are often not able to function in the working world and need a source of income. They are so traumatized by their life experiences that they often develop mental illnesses and frequently use negative coping strategies such as drugs and alcohol to bury their pain. They often become homeless due to their inability to maintain stable housing when feeding their addictions takes precedence over meeting basic needs, so they sometimes also end up depending on systems such as addiction treatment facilities, hospitals, and homeless shelters. Statistics show a high percentage of children who transition out of CFS end up in these and other systems. We will zoom in the lens to further explore this next, in Chapter 5.

PART THREE

THE SYSTEM DEPENDENCY CYCLE: WILL IT EVER CHANGE?

In this section, we will magnify what happens when children transition from the child welfare system to dependence on other systems. You will be able to see how the effects of the SAD pandemic facilitate the transition from one system directly into another. Some of the dis-services children experience in these circumstances often go unnoticed, as it has become a socially accepted idea that people who were products of the child welfare system are doomed to fall through the cracks of society.

DIFFERENT SYSTEM

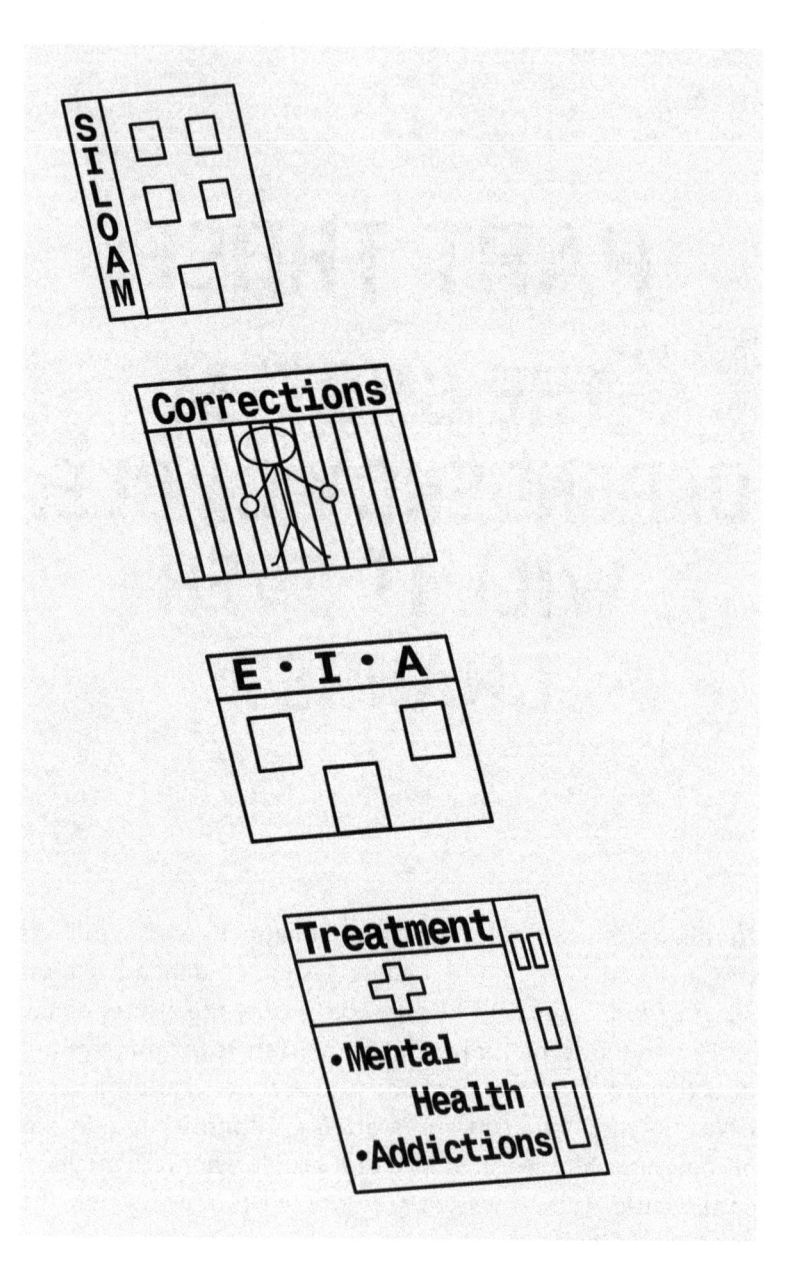

- SILOAM
- Corrections
- E·I·A
- Treatment
  - Mental Health
  - Addictions

FIVE
TRANSITIONING INTO OTHER SYSTEMS

MANY CHILDREN LEAVING care transition into different systems such as prison, the Employment and Income Assistance program, a mental health institution, a drug rehabilitation program, or homelessness. There seems to be a very strong connection between these various systems that children journey through as they transition from childhood to young adulthood. The chronology that begins on the next page depicts the profile of a typical system child, showing how such a person moves from one system to another. A combination of some or all of these might exist for a typical CFS child.

PROFILE OF A SYSTEM CHILD

- Born suffering from withdrawal symptoms from a mom who was addicted to drugs and alcohol during her pregnancy. Predisposed to a Fetal Alcohol Spectrum Disorder (FASD) diagnosis.

- Taken into care through birth alert from the hospital and struggled with attachment issues due to failed reunification attempts. Was repeatedly traumatized in this process when returned to a home which was presumed cured from the SAD pandemic.

- Use of substances to cope with negative past experiences, necessitating the use of **drug rehabilitation systems.**

- Mental Health and behavioural concerns—self-harming, suicidal ideation, and seeking an escape from CFS life realities. Use of **hospitals and mental health crisis** response facilities.

- Cognitive disabilities due to FASD diagnosis. School attendance and academic performance impacted, resulting in an inability to enter the workforce. Lack of income leads to dependency on **Employment and Income Assistance (EIA)**

- Assessments show the inability to live independently at the age of majority; therefore, transition into the **adult services system** occurs.

- At high risk for criminal involvement due to inability to control anger and to follow rules and laws, as well as a lack of understanding of cause and effect and no regard for consequences. As a result, some might end up incarcerated in either the youth or adult **prison systems.**

- Not fully prepared at the age of majority but transitioned out of care anyway, based on youth and family's demand. May become a couch surfer (**homeless**), gang leader or member, or may be exposed to sexual exploitation or become involved in the drug or sex trade (source of income).

As mentioned in our message to policymakers earlier in the book, it is not possible to look at a system's function in isolation, as systems are interconnected and interrelated. These different systems have allowed the SAD pandemic to evolve over time through many generations. Families become dependent on the child welfare system to care for their children (when struggling to meet their basic needs while living off a very low income received through EIA). The stress of poverty coupled with other underlying factors sometimes drives parents to develop mental illnesses. Additionally, due to poor coping strategies they often use drugs and alcohol. This then leads to CFS involvement where children are removed from their homes.

In order for families to improve, they now have to access addictions and mental health treatments after their children are removed. However, often when the children are gone, parents have more freedom to progress further into their addictions and develop even more mental health concerns. Additionally, EIA income decreases when children are removed from the home, which makes parents less able to afford their living expenses. Because of the system dependency syndrome that occurred when parents received money based on the number of children they had in their household; they are no longer able to afford their living expenses. With such a limited source of income, many turn to the streets, joining the sex or drug trade as an alternative source of income or to supplement the small amount of money their EIA paycheck gives them.

Therefore, instead of getting better in order to have their children returned to their care, some parents get progressively worse. The result is usually loss of housing and a downward spiral into a transient lifestyle, as well as even further progression into addictions to cope with their stress and mental illness. This leads to permanent loss of what is most important to them—their children.

Social safety net programs such as EIA and homelessness resources are initiatives that were originally implemented to catch those who fell through the cracks of society and to help them out on a short-term basis. Unfortunately, former children in care and their families are highly represented amongst the people who access these social safety nets. This often leads to the creation of a **dependency syndrome**, which continues to be perpetuated over time, leading

> **Dependency syndrome** "is an attitude and belief that a group or individual cannot solve its own problems without outside help. Charity makes this weakness worse" (Bartle P, 2012).

to the development of an **entitlement mentality**. It then becomes increasingly difficult to break away from this cycle.

> **Entitlement mentality** is "a state of mind in which an individual comes to believe that privileges are instead rights, and they often expect others to solve their problems, refusing to accept that the problems are of their own making" (Conservapedia).

Transitioning into Other Systems

✓ Employment and Income Assistance: EIA System

It is often said that children live what they learn. Therefore, if a child's parents already receive social assistance and the child grows up seeing his/her parents never going to work but still receiving a paycheck, he/she might not develop the motivation to enter the workforce when he/she gets older. Children might end up becoming dependent on receiving a paycheck from their EIA worker, as this behaviour has become normalized.

This is the same if the child becomes a ward of the child welfare system. The agency, which is their legal guardian, cannot change this mentality. During age of majority planning, when children get to their teenage years, they receive an independent living paycheck biweekly without having to work for it. For example, when one worker sat down to case plan with a teen approaching the age of majority, the teen explained that she would prefer to go on welfare instead of getting into the workforce.

Even at a program level, this type of mentality continues. One transition planning program's mandate stipulates that youths should be trained to operate under an EIA budget, as this is typically what they will receive after they leave the child welfare system. Thus, when removed from families that relied on EIA paychecks, some children end up continuing the cycle of EIA dependency, even though they were taken into care to experience a different way of life which would hopefully break the cycle of poverty that existed in their family of origin. It is very difficult to accept that children who become a part of the child welfare system have become so stigmatized that society expects them to continue to rely on the services of social safety net programs.

Looking through a social justice lens, it leaves one to wonder if we do a dis-service to children when we automatically transition them into welfare dependence instead of encouraging them to independently transition into the workforce. What kind of messages are we sending to the young people who will shape the future of their home and native land? In order to break this cycle of system dependency, there should be more supports in place. The children's workers might need to place more emphasis on advocating to policy makers for resources so that their CIC can benefit from skill development. This might lead to more CIC being encouraged and empowered to join the workforce upon their age of majority.

✓ Mental Health and Addiction Facilities: Health and Treatment Systems

Children impacted by the SAD pandemic usually need mental health supports because they tend to develop mental health issues related to trauma and substance abuse. A genetic predisposition for mental illness can also be a factor. When triggered by environmental trauma such as sexual violence, addictions, and domestic violence (SAD), children go into crisis mode and need emergency mental health services from psychealth centres such as Manitoba Adolescent Treatment Centre (MATC).

The mental health journey for some of the CFS children started in utero. The expectant mother often has stressful relationships with unhealthy people in an environment plagued by domestic violence. She might have even experienced sexual violence, which may have resulted in unplanned and teenage pregnancies. Also, many pregnant mothers use drugs and alcohol to cope with their stressful situations. This practice impacts the fetus during the early stages of pregnancy, as alcohol destroys and damages cells in the central nervous system of the developing baby/fetus. The mother may continue the lifestyle of addiction throughout her pregnancy.

Therefore, such a child might be born suffering from withdrawal or predisposed to FASD due to alcohol exposure in utero. Research has shown that fetal alcohol and drug exposure poses cognitive/developmental and behavioral challenges during childhood, so this may cause the child to feel socially isolated because they are different from their peers. In addition, most of these children develop self-esteem issues which can lead to self-harming and running away from home. And some children may fall through the cracks within the system if their mothers do not disclose that they used substances during pregnancy.

As these children get older, their risk for drug use and suicidal ideation increases. Some develop drug-induced mental illnesses resulting from the use of substances such as crystal meth, fentanyl, cocaine, and marijuana. Psychosis and schizophrenia due to drug use initiates a referral to mental health and addiction facilities such as Youth Addictions Stabilization Unit (YASU), Crisis Stabilization Unit (CSU), Behavioural Health Foundation (BHF), and Addictions Foundation of Manitoba (AFM).

✓ Adult Services is one of the systems that the children transition into as a result of the effects of SAD on their mental and emotional development. The provincial government mandates that social workers provide access to adult services resources to children preparing to transition out of the child welfare system. The children who were already traumatized and displayed mental health concerns would qualify for such a service. Due to the effects of SAD on their cognitive and emotional development, they usually score very low on their IQ test and other assessments. Additionally, the impact of trauma, alcohol, and drugs on their social, emotional, and cognitive development impairs their social functioning and their ability to successfully transition out of care into living independently. Instead of going into independent living, they go into "dependent living"—Community Living Disability Services (CLDS). These facilities provide the necessary supports to meet their needs.

✓ Youth and Adult Correction Facilities: Prison System

Some children affected by the SAD pandemic have early exposure to and interaction with the justice system. Children experience the trauma of police intervention in neighborhoods that law enforcement officers frequent due to gang or drug activities. Also, police sometimes must assist when children need protection and are removed from their homes.

Due to SAD, parents are either usually under the influence of substances, very angry, and/or violent towards the child protection workers or towards each other when protection interventions occur. Police assistance is then required to make the process of removal incident-free. Connection with the justice system during these traumatic events may result in children becoming very angry at law enforcement personnel. Therefore, the safety of the children and the workers is sometimes jeopardized in the removal process.

Additionally, these children see law enforcement personnel very often responding to the various side effects of SAD:

- Responding to domestic violence calls
- Cruising neighborhoods to ensure safety
- Coming into their family homes, foster placements, and group homes to respond to their behavioral issues. For example, de-escalating and restraining them when they are aggressive towards their peers and caregivers, taking them to crisis units when they make suicide attempts,

and searching to locate and return them when they run away. Police assistance is also required when children end up in places such as drug houses also known as "trap houses". Sometimes officers must arrest children and take them to youth or adult correctional facilities when they commit crimes. If the youths breach their probation conditions, they are re-arrested, thus starting the cycle of repeatedly returning to the justice system.

It is a well-known fact that a close relationship exists between the child welfare system and the justice system. A recent review of admissions at the Manitoba Youth Centre showed about 60% of youth charged were also involved with child welfare services (*CBC* Feb 15, 2019). Oftentimes these youths then end up graduating to the adult correctional system.

✓ Homeless Resource Systems

In Canada, there are shelters and housing initiatives at both the community and government levels in response to homelessness. We have seen where the SAD pandemic played a role in a child's journey towards depending on these resources. Children who have experience with child protection represent a high percentage of homeless youths.

A pilot project that looked at the correlation between the child welfare system and youth homelessness in Canada mentioned that "research has shown over-representation of both youth and adults with a history of care among the homeless in the US, Canada, and the UK" (Serge et al., 2002, 9). From the presented facts, there is no doubt that a correlation exists between child welfare and homelessness.

The above illustrated system dependency and homelessness further reveals itself in the 2013/2014 Systems Pathways into Homelessness research conducted by the Social Planning Council of Winnipeg, Resources for Adolescence and Youth (RAY), and the University of Winnipeg. This study indicates that not only do some children leave the child welfare system and go directly into homelessness, but some might also take a longer journey towards homelessness.

When youth enter the prison system while they are in care or close to the age of majority, sometimes they lose their CFS status when they reach their age of majority in the process of serving their sentences for serious offences. These youths, when released from jail, have no legal guardian because they are now adults, and with nowhere to go after completing their prison sentence, they end up on the streets or dependent upon accessing homeless shelters. They therefore leave from the prison system into homelessness. Because they are homeless, some might reoffend and return to prison, where they are guaranteed to get what one youth called "three hots and a cot."

Being in and out of jail becomes the norm for many of our youths who have given up hope of ever bouncing back into functioning well socially. Unless these young adults can get accepted into one of the homeless facilities, such as Siloam Mission, they might not get the opportunity to ever function as independent citizens.

In perspective, the Siloam Mission has been a pivotal institution in addressing homelessness among youth who exit care. Through their Exit Up Program, many former youths in care benefit from this intervention, which helps them break the cycle. Likewise, in Ontario, the Children's Aid Society's Pape Adolescent Resource Centre (PARC) program assists youth in the transition to adulthood, recognizing that youth exiting care face many challenge and difficulties.

Unless it becomes a financial and/or safety concern for the entire society, many will remain silent on the issue of the

SAD pandemic. We can already see that the issue has become a financial problem. A study in Manitoba has shown that a person with FASD will cost the system an estimated $800,000 more than the average Canadian over their lifetime. The $800,000 cost will be distributed between sectors including: healthcare (30%), education (24%), social services (19%), justice (14%), and other (13%) (*Child and Youth Report* 2017).

When the SAD pandemic surpasses a limit where just one system can no longer contain it, it finds a way to extend itself and seep into other systems. Thus, we have to wonder if our country will have a bright future when this becomes a social norm. A child leaving the child welfare system, suffering from all the deficits outlined in his/her journey towards dependence on other systems, is in a sad state. As a society, are we willing to take action to break this vicious cycle?

To provide you with a clear picture of the system dependency cycle, let us follow the life journey of a typical CFS child navigating in between and through the different social systems:

• • •

John White shared his testimony in a CBC News article, posted on February 07, 2019. He attended an event hosted by the Siloam Mission Homelessness Initiative Shelter Expansion Program, and he said at the event that Siloam made a difference for him when he first came to Winnipeg from Alberta thirteen years ago.

"I've been down the road of being homeless. I've been down the road of addiction. I've been down the road of just not having anyone in my life," White said. "I've started this journey at birth—I was homeless; I was in 21 different foster homes. I came to Siloam for support."

• • •

SIX
THE CYCLE CONTINUES. WHO IS TO BLAME?

IT IS INDEED a dis-service when social abnormalities like SAD do not get the attention they truly deserve. In this last chapter, we will zoom in the lens to look at some of the issues that need the attention of policymakers. These issues should take top priority on Canada's political agenda—and not only on the political agenda but also on TV and radio stations, to bring about public awareness and be a constant reminder to us as Canadian citizens.

Looking at outcomes based on the current situation of the SAD pandemic, we reviewed an article M.D. Brownell wrote in December 2011 entitled "Children in Care and Child Maltreatment in Manitoba: What Does Research from the Manitoba Centre for Health Policy Tell Us, and Where Do We Go from Here?" Brownell prepared this paper for Phase

III of the Phoenix Sinclair Inquiry. Based on our professional experience in the field, this research, and other studies we have reviewed, we need to address the SAD pandemic because it puts the future of the children at risk. The study pointed out that, generally, the outcomes for children in care are usually poor. Brownell stated that, "It is however difficult to tell whether or not the poorer outcomes experienced by children in care are as a result of being in care itself, or if these poorer outcomes are caused by the factors that led to the children being in care" (Brownell 2011, 9). Based on our experience in the field, the main factor that causes children to be in care is the SAD pandemic.

Compared to other countries in the world, research shows that Canada has one of the highest rates of children in care, including the province of Manitoba (Brownell 2011, 8). With this in mind, we will now give you a snapshot of the statistics, so you will have a clearer picture of what the outcomes look like for these children.

The number of children in care in Manitoba gets increasingly higher on a yearly basis. Data pre- and post-child welfare devolution show a gradual increase in the number of children who have entered the child welfare system over the past fifteen years post-devolution. In the Manitoba Family Services and Housing Annual Report dated 2003-2004, there were 5,782 children in care. Eight years later, statistics from the Annual Report of Manitoba Family Services and Consumer Affairs (now Manitoba Family Services and Labour) revealed that there were 9,432 children in care as of March 31, 2011. The most current statistics are from September 2018, when the province released a snapshot of its year-end report. According to the report, there were 10,328 children in care as of March 31—down by 3% from 2017.

Number of past CIC on welfare: 9% to 33.5% of former youths in care who are between the ages of eighteen and nineteen years old received income assistance as young adults (Brownell 2011, 4).

Number of past CIC not fully educated: When looking at the educational outcomes for children involved in the child welfare system, we reviewed existing data from the Manitoba Centre for Health and Policy. As Brownell (2011) noted in her research paper, for youths whose only risk factor was receiving services from CFS, 57.2% of them completed high school within seven years of entering grade nine, compared to 81.9% of youths who did not have this as a risk factor (4). The educational outcomes are poorer for children who had experience in care.

Number of past CIC ending up homeless: The Social Planning Council of Winnipeg conducted a study looking at the problem of homelessness in the city of Winnipeg. This study pointed out that the number of former youths in care who become homeless is of concern. Cameron Maclean, reporting on the matter, mentioned that the Winnipeg street census revealed that close to two-thirds of respondents who had been involved with CFS became homeless within a year of leaving care (*CBC* Oct. 10, 2018).

Number of past CIC ending up in the prison system: Again, the spotlight shines on Manitoba, which has the highest incarceration rate in Canada. Youth in care account for 60% of those at the Manitoba Youth Centre. Minister of Justice Cliff Cullen stated, "that there is a link between persons who are involved with the child and family service system and the criminal justice system" (*Global News* May 10, 2019).

For a broader view across Canada, we looked over data that was gathered for a comparative study in 1988. We saw that the problem of SAD has continued to affect the lives of children for over three decades. Before the twentieth century and thereafter, many research studies have shown how SAD has affected the children whose families have exposed them to it for many generations. A pilot project that looked at the link between the child welfare system and youth homelessness in Canada focused on the initial trauma that caused children to be removed from their families and placed in the child welfare system. The study revealed that the "foster care system often fails to help (some) children with the problems that resulted from circumstances that caused them to be removed from their homes in the first place (for example, physical or sexual abuse, parents with alcohol or substance abuse, and family dissolution)" (Serge et al. 2002, 11).

What do the studies show?

Removing children from their homes does not necessarily solve this problem. If we do not address the impact of SAD, then we will continue to have children who exhibit poor outcomes. The solution to the problem is not necessarily removing children from SAD situations. The solution to the problem is addressing SAD from its root. A study done by Serge, Eberle, Goldberg, Sullivan, and Dudding in 2002 compared children who were not traumatized by SAD in their homes to children who were exposed to SAD. The study revealed that children who were exposed to SAD had poor outcomes whether or not they were removed from their homes into foster care. The study then posed the question: "Why doesn't the child welfare system do a better job?"

The authors of this book concur that, although we still need the child welfare system, the focus of the system needs to change to address the SAD pandemic directly. The solution to the problem is to fix SAD because removing children from their homes and putting them in the child welfare system until they emancipate at their age of majority does not provide a solution to the SAD pandemic that is so rampant here in Canada.

The comparative study done in 1988 and the study done by Serge, Eberle, Goldberg, Sullivan, and Dudding in 2002 have a fourteen-year time gap. Despite the time gap, their outcomes still point to the same or common problem—SAD. In our country, it is easy to blame the child welfare system for these poor outcomes, but we fail to realize that what we really need to do is get to the root cause of the trauma, that is, the SAD pandemic. Are we willing to continue this downward spiral, or are we going to take action to treat or eradicate the SAD pandemic in order to break this cycle?

After all, it is a long time to wait to realize that if a treatment is not found for SAD, the future of our children is at risk. Will we continue to perpetuate a dis-service to children and families while SAD feeds children into systems and situations where there is:

I. Cash for kids exchange

II. System dependencies and entitlement mentalities

III. Intergenerational involvement in CFS

These outcomes beg the question, "who is to blame?"

RECOMMENDATIONS

In Chapter 1, we looked at child welfare in the past and how it has evolved into its current form. Throughout the book, we have taken you on a journey into the current child welfare system and highlighted the impact of the SAD pandemic on children and families who are part of it. We have shown you how these deficiencies have led to dependency on other systems, and we have wondered whether this system dependency cycle will ever change. Now, we will explore what the future of child welfare could look like if we would move forward in a positive way instead of repeating the past and recycling what is happening presently.

- ✓ **Focus on Parental Accountability.** While it is every parent's right to procreate in order to continue human society, it is even more important that parents are held accountable for the responsibility of raising their children to become fully functioning members of society who will contribute to the growth and development of their country. *According to Article 18 of the United Nations Convention on the Rights of the Child:*

1. States Parties shall use their best efforts to ensure recognition of the principle that both parents have common responsibilities for the upbringing and development of the child. Parents or legal guardians have the primary responsibility for the upbringing and development of the child. The best interests of the child will be their basic concern.

2. For the purpose of guaranteeing and promoting the rights set forth in the present Convention, States Parties shall render appropriate assistance to parents and legal guardians in the performance of their child-rearing responsibilities and shall ensure the development of institutions, facilities and services for the care of children.

With this being said, let us focus on some practical strategies that can be used to enforce Article 18 of the Convention on the Rights of the Child:

1. Parent training: Instead of denying parents the opportunity to carry out their inherent responsibility, that is, to take care of their children, it would be better to support them in the process of doing their job. Parenting is indeed a full-time job, and every job requires that a person receive on-the-job training so that they can successfully do their job. Also, a person's resume must prove that they are qualified to do the job before someone hires them to do it. How awesome it would be if parents could make it a priority to first

attend parenting classes to get themselves trained and qualified. After having confidence that the parenting training they have received qualifies them to become successful at parenting, then they can make the decision to enter the child-rearing workforce.

When employees face challenges that hinder job performance and positive outcomes, they receive an evaluation to assist them with strengthening their skills in the areas where they need improvements. If, after they receive the support to improve their job performance, they still do not improve, the employer takes them through a disciplinary process that may ultimately lead to job loss. Parents should not lose their job because this is a job that everyone should work very hard at keeping. However, if the pressure becomes too much and a parent feels like abandoning their post and leaving their children at risk, then they need a replacement, as the job of taking care of the child is something that **MUST** be done. If the child's own parents are not willing to do the job, an alternative caregiver must be found, be it a family member, relative, community member, or strangers who have a heart to do the job, whether they will be highly compensated or not.

2. Investing in treatment programs where parents could continue their parental duties and responsibilities while they recover: Look at the existing treatment models such as Behavioral Health Foundation (BHF). How could we make these programs more family-inclusive so that parents could have their children with them, fulfilling their responsibilities with little to no interruptions in the children's regular lives or routines. A school bus could transport children from the treatment

facilities to school for the period that they and their parents stay at the facilities.

3. Creating alternative models that shift from child welfare to parental accountability: This would require a thorough evaluation using a cost-benefit perspective. It may be prudent to have pilot programs that will be studied and evaluated, with results compared over time.

✓ From Devolution to Resolution.

If we would partner to develop a child welfare model that would work post-devolution, it could be used as a training curriculum across the provinces and territories. It is the intention of the federal government to devolve child welfare in Canada. Seeing that Manitoba has already had a devolved child welfare system in place for the past fifteen years, can we look to Manitoba as a best practice model? If so, it would make sense to do a review, assessment, and evaluation that focuses on:

- The similarities and differences in child welfare practices of the four Authorities and their culturally appropriate agencies

- The specific service delivery models used in different Authorities

- Successes or lessons learned since devolution in Manitoba over the past fifteen years

- The implementation of best practice training modules across all four Authorities as part of a provincial standard of practice in order to bring about consistency in service delivery models

Recommendations

- Appreciative Inquiry—As a strategic planning model to engage all stakeholders when planning the future of the agency (General Authority)

- Andrew Turnell—Signs of Safety approach to assess the safety and risk of children and families (Metis Authority)

   The Signs of Safety approach to child protection casework was developed through the 1990s in Western Australia. It was created by Andrew Turnell and Steve Edwards, in collaboration with over 150 West Australian child protection workers (CPWs), and is now utilized in jurisdictions in the USA, Canada, the UK, Sweden, the Netherlands, New Zealand, and Japan. The approach focuses on the question "How can the worker build partnerships with parents and children in situations of suspected or substantiated child abuse and still deal rigorously with the maltreatment issues?" (https://www.signsofsafety.net/signs-of-safety/)

✓ **Inter-provincial government agreements** to support paying for resources used by individuals who migrate to other provinces

✓ **Focus on preventative intervention by treating the SAD pandemic from the root:** Finding a cure for SAD and replacing it with JOY.

CHILD AND FAMILY DIS-SERVICES

CONCLUSION

We have taken you on a journey where you were able to look through a social justice lens at the child welfare system, and we magnified the problem of the SAD pandemic and its impact on children and families. Now we will conclude this book by asking you to reflect on the following questions:

1. What type of future is the village creating?
2. Are we willing to help break the cycle in order to have a brighter future?

You might be tempted to tell yourself, "it is not my problem, and after all, I am not the one to blame for the SAD pandemic." But the reality is that, as citizens of this country, it impacts all of us, whether directly or indirectly. Our joint efforts are needed to combat the SAD monster that plagues our society and takes over the lives of children who are the future of our country. It is a battle we must win. Let us join forces to win this battle against SAD by replacing it with JOY (A holistic approach that helps individuals to organize themselves to live a fulfilled life). To experience JOY view the final page in this book and join our community today. There is a hero inside of us all. We can join forces with these superheroes and take action to seek justice for the future of children.

Let us all work together to *save the children.*

Let us: (1) Go back to where the village raised the children.
(2) Get rid of SAD, which allows children to be fed into the CFS system.
(3) Stop recycling children from one system to another.

This can only be possible if we all become radical in our efforts to bring about the needed change. If not you, who will save the children? All it takes to make this change is to start with the man in the mirror. If the man in the mirror is willing to love his neighbor as himself, if the man in the mirror is willing to seek justice, love mercy, and walk humbly, then he can bring out the hero inside of him and be a world changer—not changing the whole world but changing a child's world.

APPENDIX

Social Work Tutor

January 10 at 7:21 PM.

Dear social worker,

You've stepped over my threshold one million times.

You've been brand new and eager and I've witnessed you worn out and oh so jaded.

You've carried me new babies fresh from the local hospital.

You've dropped confused big kids in my foyer at 3am too.

I've seen the look of desperation in your eyes from all the calls you've made asking for someone, ANYONE, to open up a bed and take in this troubled teen.

I've even embraced you in tears as you allowed the weight of your nineteen-hour day to be released right there on my living room floor.

You've juggled dirty diaper bags and trash bags filled with the only clothing you could find for this child.

You've whispered stories of egregious abuse and painful pasts in the doorway of my home.

I'm familiar with the insecurities you ignore as you pull into my driveway for the first time.

You don't know me but our worlds are about to collide in the most intimate and sacred of ways.

We aren't sure if we'll love each other or be annoyed because of all the questions and unmet expectations.

We are certain to disappoint one another and do our fair share of frustrating on more than one occasion.

But what stands between us, what we are both fighting for, is worth the collateral damage of the relationship we're entering into.

I choose to believe that our hearts are headed in the same direction.

We both stepped into the wreckage of child welfare because we wanted to advocate for all of the abandoned, abused and neglected innocents of our community.

We both want kids safe, needs met, feeling loved.

And with my advocating of a kid comes my public proclamation of my support for you.

Appendix

I bet people don't know you stood in the Wal-Mart checkout line for twenty minutes (because they always only have ONE register open) to purchase a box of diapers for the child you're about to place.

Those things are expensive. Legit.

You make barely enough to feed yourself and pay your own bills. But you do it anyway.

You grabbed a Dr. Pepper and a bag of chips because dinner was four hours ago and you still haven't eaten.

You also missed your best friend's birthday party because you were transporting a sibling group of three to a weekly visit in another city.

You've filled your car up twice this week and you're almost on empty again.

You're empty in so many spaces because you're pouring everything into someone else.

Your sacrifice is often unseen and unshared.

Looming over your head are the regulations to be followed and violations of HIPPA to dance around.

You wonder if you should have said this or that to parents and relatives, and even me.

Paperwork is exhausting your every encounter.

Deadlines for judicial reviews and home studies and referrals and all the other things threaten to force your hand on resigning from it all.

And then there's the heartache of your own attachment to kids in care.

Sure, you drop them off at a new mama's house, but you come to love them and know them too.

Foster parents aren't the only ones wishing things were different.

You serve as chauffeur, therapist, advocate and only friend.

You hate glancing in the backseat at the timid faces on their way to visit parents who have caused nothing but chaos in their little lives.

You are drowning in the devastation and it's all you never dreamed it would be.

You wanted to change the world and now the world is changing you.

You breathe in the bombardment of trauma and try to live life like your neighbors but you can't unseen your everyday etchings.

Here's the part I hate the most.

When something goes horribly wrong, like death post-reunification or a child taking his own life because of the trauma you couldn't save him from, people want to blame you.

They don't know. They've never seen.

They can't possibly understand how sometimes your heart's cry to stand in the gap falls on the deaf ears of supposed justice.

Your hands are tied by legislation you can't change but must obey.

Appendix

I know you're doing the best you can.

I see you stepping in and standing alone sometimes.

I know people don't get it, but don't stop.

You have shown me how to be brave and fight hard and love big.

You have been written into the lines of so many stories-including my own.

You stood, tears streaming, on the day of our adoption because you were with us on the battlefield day after day.

You cheered and celebrated the permanency of one more child.

So keep fielding phone calls and late night texts about placement disruptions and runaway teens.

Keep stepping into the s***show of it all because we need what you're doing.

We see your sacrifice and I personally am giving you a standing ovation over here.

Thanks for putting up with my knee-jerk reactions to the insanity of co-parenting.

Thanks for tolerating every eye roll and deep sigh I toss your way.

Dear social worker, I'll keep saying yes WITH you and together we will protect and press on and defend and do what's right.

And when you're ready to walk away, remember all the good you've done, all the lives you've loved and all the places you've walked into that no one else was courageous enough to discover.

You are doing the toughest work and for that, this foster mama is forever grateful.

-Kristy Sutton (foster mama)

BIBLIOGRAPHY

A Place Where It Feels Like Home: The Story of Tina Fontaine. Winnipeg: Manitoba Advocate, March 2019.

Bala, Bala, Nicholas, Michael K. Zapf, R. James William, Robin Vogl, and Joseph Hornick. *Canadian Child Welfare Law: Children, Families and the State.* 2nd ed. Toronto Thompson Educational Publishing, Inc., 2004.

Bartle, Phil. "The Dependency Syndrome." CEC Community Empowerment Collective. Last modified June 11, 2012. http://cec.vcn.bc.ca/cmp/modules/pd-dep.htm.

Brownell, Marni D. "Children in Care and Child Maltreatment in Manitoba: What Does Research From the Manitoba Centre for Health Policy Tell Us, and Where Do We Go From Here?" Commission of Inquiry into the Circumstances Surrounding the

Death of Phoenix Sinclair. Dec. 1, 2011. http://phoenixsinclairinquiry.ca/exhibits/exhibit139.pdf.

CBC. "Manitoba to look at connection between youth incarceration and child welfare." Feb 15, 2019. https://www.cbc.ca/news/canada/manitoba/youth-justice-child-welfare-manitoba-1.5021229.

CBC. "More options than the street: Siloam Mission in home stretch of $19M expansion." Feb 7, 2019. https://www.cbc.ca/news/canada/manitoba/siloam-mission-expansion-update-1.5010144.

CBC. "Youth homelessness linked to foster care system in new study." August 9, 2017. https://www.cbc.ca/news/health/homeless-youth-foster-care-1.4240121.

Child and Youth Report. Winnipeg: Healthy Child Manitoba, 2017. https://www.gov.mb.ca/healthychild/publications/hcm_2017report.pdf.

City News. "Manitoba to look at connection between youth incarceration and child welfare." February 15, 2019. https://toronto.citynews.ca/2019/02/15/manitoba-to-look-at-connection-between-youth-incarceration-and-child-welfare/.

Conservapedia. "Entitlement Mentality." https://www.conservapedia.com/Entitlement_mentality.

Courtney, Mark, Christina Maes Nino, and Evelyn Peters. *System Pathways Into Youth Homelessness.* 2014. http://www.hereandnowwinnipeg.ca/wp-content/uploads/2016/09/SystemPathways-SPCW-2014.pdf.

Dictionary.com. "Pandemic." https://www.dictionary.com/browse/pandemic.

Dictionary.com. "Systems." https://www.dictionary.com/browse/system.

Global News. "Manitoba reducing number of people in jail, still has highest prison rates." May 10, 2019. https://globalnews.ca/news/5263856/

manitoba-reducing-number-of-people-in-jail-still-has-highest-prison-rates/.

Hobson, Brittany. "Number of children in care in Manitoba down, but grand chief says province can do better." *APTN National News*, September 26, 2018. https://aptnnews.ca/2018/09/26/number-of-children-in-care-in-manitoba-down-but-grand-chief-says-province-can-do-better/.

Homeless Hub. n.d. "Foster Care." Accessed June 20, 2019. https://www.homelesshub.ca/about-homelessness/legal-justice-issues/foster-care.

Kaur, Raveet and Suneela Garg. "Addressing Domestic Violence Against Women: An Unfinished Agenda." *Indian Journal of Community Medicine* 33 (2008): 2. https://www.ncbi.nlm.nih.gov/pmc/articles/PMC2784629/ doi: 10.4103/0970-0218.40871.

MacLean, Cameron. "Homeless census highlights need for support for youth in care, Indigenous people, organizer says." *CBC*, October 10, 2018. http://www.cbc.ca/news/canada/manitoba/homeless-census-winnipeg-2018-1.4856548.

Province of Manitoba. "Child and Family Services Overview and Statistics." https://gov.mb.ca/fs/childfam/investments.html.

Province of Manitoba. *Manitoba Family Services and Housing Annual Report 2003-2004*. September, 2004. https://www.gov.mb.ca/fs/about/annual_reports/2003-04/annual_2003-04.pdf.

Rycus, Judith, and Ron Hughes. *Child Welfare Values and Principles Put into Practice: From Ancient Egypt to the Twenty-First Century*. Institute for Human Services: Columbus, OH, 2004. http://www.ocwtp.net/PDFs/Trainee%20Resources/Skill-Building%20Resources/CW%201%20Pre.pdf.

Serge, L. Uba, Margaret Eberle, Michael Goldberg, Susan Sullivan, and Peter Duddin. *The Child Welfare System and Homelessness Among Canadian Youth*. Ottawa Canada System, 2002. https://www.homelesshub. ca/sites/default/files/attachments/Pilot_Study_The_ Child_Welfare_System_and_Homelessness.pdf.

Sinha, Vandna and Anna Kozlowski. "The Structure of Aboriginal Child Welfare in Canada." *The International Indigenous Policy Journal* 4 (2013): 2. http://ir.lib.uwo. ca/iipj/vol4/iss2/2 DOI:10.18584/iipj.2013.4.2.2.

The Free Dictionary. "Do somebody a disservice." https://idioms.thefreedictionary.com/ do+somebody+a+disservice.

The Legacy of Phoenix Sinclair, Achieving the Best for All Our Children, Vol 2, Dec 2013 http://www. phoenixsinclairinquiry.ca/rulings/ps_volume2.pdf.

Turnell, Andrew and Steve Edwards "Signs of Safety Approach" https://www.signsofsafety.net/ signs-of-safety/.

United Nations Convention of the Rights of the Child (Sep 1990) https://www.ohchr.org/en/ professionalinterest/pages/crc.aspx.

Vocabulary.com. "Colonization." https://www.vocabulary. com/dictionary/colonazation.

Wikipedia: The Free Encyclopedia. "Villain." https:// en.wikipedia.org/wiki/Villain.

Cynthia Eyeshemitan

Cynthia has a master's degree and a bachelor's degree in social work. She is a registered social worker with over ten years of experience working in the child welfare system in Manitoba. Her parents, grandparents, great-grandmother, relatives, and community members in a village in Nigeria, West Africa raised Cynthia. She has firsthand experience of "the village raising the child" and is an ardent believer in the importance of a culture and village raising children. Cynthia's passion for taking care of people in her community where she saw great needs led her to pursue a career in the helping profession. Cynthia has a heart that reaches out to help children and their families.

In addition, she has worked with thousands of youth struggling with a wide range of issues such as childhood trauma, unresolved attachment issues, addictions, gang involvement, anger problems, gambling, school attendance, and human trafficking. She is a strong advocate for youth programs.

Cynthia is a proud recipient of a 2009 Youth Role Model Award from the Citizen Equity Committee of Winnipeg.

Cynthia has previous writing experience through the many academic research papers she has written throughout her undergraduate and graduate level studies. Cynthia wrote her academic papers on topics such as homelessness, child sexual abuse, domestic violence, policy analysis and the history of child welfare, policies, program design and evaluation, evaluability assessment, and individual counseling.

Colleen McCaulsky

Colleen has a Master of Social Work (MSW) and is a qualified and registered social worker with approximately five years of experience working in the child welfare system in Manitoba, Canada. Colleen has assisted with raising and caring for many children as their biological auntie and also as an elementary school teacher. With a heart and a passion to see children reach their full potential, Colleen made a change in her career path to assist in addressing the social needs of the children in her community in Kingston, Jamaica. Colleen embarked on a career in social work, as she wanted to be a support to children and their families. Colleen is also a strong believer in the concept of "it takes a village to raise a child" and has been playing a pivotal role in making a positive impact on the lives of the children and families she has supported for over twenty years.

Colleen has previous writing experience in both her graduate and undergraduate studies where she wrote academic papers in the area of youth involvement in the justice system. Colleen also wrote about working with individuals and families using different therapeutic interventions to bring about positive behaviour changes.

Kareen has a Master of Social Work (MSW) and is a qualified and registered social worker with approximately ten years of experience working in the Manitoba child welfare system. Kareen is able to identify with the concept of the village raising the child based on her own experience of being raised by her neighbour during her teenage years. Born in one of the poor inner-city communities in Kingston, Jamaica, Kareen knows what it is like to live in a community where people take care of each other's children as they would take care of their own children. Kareen spent her early childhood with her mother and father and then lived with her neighbour and her neighbour's husband throughout her adolescent years. Kareen had both her biological grandmother and aunties and also community "grandmas" and "aunties" who shaped and molded her into the woman she has become: a social worker with a heart and passion to love and care for children and their families.

Kareen's previous writing experience was done at an academic level both during her undergraduate and graduate studies. Kareen's papers focused on issues such as education, poverty, and homelessness.

Kareen Thompson

Be a Part of The VOV

The Voice of Voiceless (The VOV) was created for people who have:
- Worked with individuals and families
- Lived with children and families
- Lost individuals and families
- Experienced injustice
- Experienced SAD in their lives and are interested in experiencing JOY

What is The Voice of Voiceless (The VOV)?

The VOV consists of passionate individuals who wish to participate in the learning and sharing journey of changing SAD to JOY. JOY is a holistic approach geared toward helping people organize their total wellbeing by addressing the physical, emotional, spiritual, mental, and psychosocial traumas that cause people to be in the SAD cycle.

We believe that in every SAD situation in life there is still hope. This group was created as a medium to work together to bridge the gap of distress and injustice as well as to provide a voice to the voiceless.

Authors of this book are available to visit universities, agencies, and to give media interviews.

Contact us for availability and join the Voice of Voiceless to experience JOY:

SCHEDULE APPOINTMENT
Email: thevov30@gmail.com
Facebook Messenger: Voice of voiceless- The VOV

JOIN OUR COMMUNITY TODAY
Website: **thevov.org**

Want to Experience JOY?

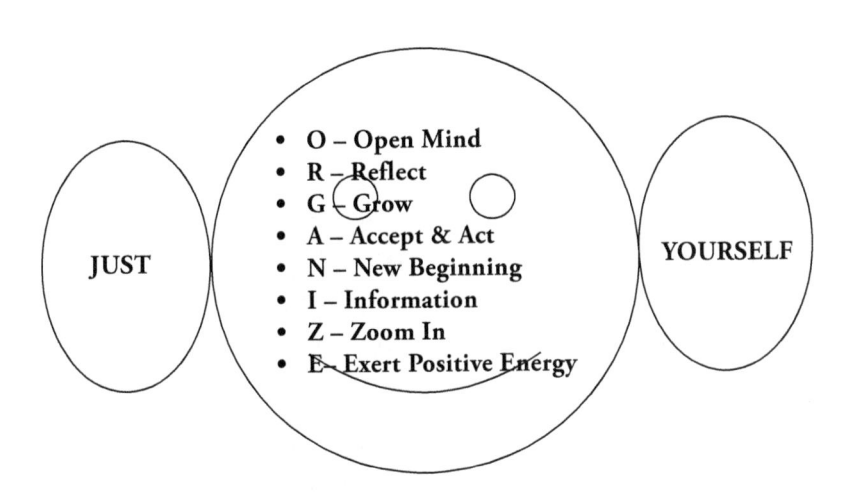

JUST
- O – Open Mind
- R – Reflect
- G – Grow
- A – Accept & Act
- N – New Beginning
- I – Information
- Z – Zoom In
- E – Exert Positive Energy

YOURSELF

This unique program allows our audience to benefit from our powerful training curriculum through one-on-one coaching or group workshops.

Stay Tuned For The Other Books In This Series

Child and Family Dis-services: Who Will Save the Children?
Child and Family Dis-services: It Takes a Village to Raise a Child
Child and Family Dis-services: Who Will Train the Workers?